IN SEARCH OF A BETTER LIFE

IN SEARCH OF A BETTER LIFE

A Doctor's Journey of Entrepreneurship at the Last Mile

Dr Sayantani Bhattacharjee

EXCELLER BOOKS®
A GLOBAL PRESS

IN SEARCH OF A BETTER LIFE

A Doctor's Journey of Entrepreneurship at the Last Mile

Cover by Tales Talks Walks

ISBN: 978-93-48892-14-0

First published in India in 2025 by Exceller Books,
An imprint of GE Group
Address: G1, Dream Apartment, Degree College Road, Belgharia,
Kolkata, 700056, India
www.excellerbooks.com

EXCELLER BOOKS®
A GLOBAL PRESS

IN SEARCH OF A BETTER LIFE

A Doctor's Journey of Entrepreneurship at the Last Mile

Dr Sayantani Bhattacharjee

EXCELLER BOOKS®
A GLOBAL PRESS

IN SEARCH OF A BETTER LIFE

A Doctor's Journey of Entrepreneurship at the Last Mile

Cover by Tales Talks Walks

ISBN: 978-93-48892-14-0

First published in India in 2025 by Exceller Books,
An imprint of GE Group
Address: G1, Dream Apartment, Degree College Road, Belgharia,
Kolkata, 700056, India
www.excellerbooks.com

EXCELLER BOOKS®
A GLOBAL PRESS

Dedicated to

Dearest Kanha!

Thank you for protecting and loving me unconditionally

I love you to the moon and back!

Acknowledgement

Thank you Saheli Mitra, my editor for listening to me so patiently. You have been my lighthouse through this entire journey of rolling out the book. It always seemed extremely overwhelming to me otherwise.

My humble gratitude to my parents….Maa & Baba….for instilling in me strong values and ethics….these became my greatest support on crossroads of life and even during tumultuous times. Also, thank you for leaving my hand….a little too soon though; my solo flights have made my wings stronger!

To my furry daughter Chiku…..you gifted me with Motherhood!

I also want to take this opportunity to thank my favourite teachers - Mrs Veena Suri, who was my classteacher in school. She nurtured me with immense love and care when my shoulders were overburdened with parental expectations.

And…Prof Ujjal Kumar Roy, under whose aegis I learnt gynaecology and obstetrics. He was not only my mentor but also an inspiration to look up to.

Thank you Amalesh Sarkar, my colleague during my tea garden days and a younger brother thereafter. The seed of Better Life was sown during the innumerable chats that we enjoyed over cups of tea, after work.

My sincere gratitude to Montu Baruah, my colleague during the Guwahati hospital days. Thank you for listening to all my crazy ideas every day. Our brainstorming sessions were absolutely critical in the making of Better Life.

A big shoutout to my team members in Better Life, especially the first team of 9 members - you people will always remain special to me. Thank you for believing in me and my vision.

And last, but not the least, my sincere gratitude to those people in my life who have doubted my abilities and have chosen to leave.....your "choice" gave me the freedom to be "me"!

Preface

This book is about a phenomenal doctor, a doctor with a heart, whose mission since her medical college days was to take affordable medical services to the last mile. In a vast country like India where remote rural areas do not even have proper roads and electricity, proper healthcare infrastructure is a far cry. That's where the author Dr Sayantani Bhattacharjee stepped in while working in the remote tea gardens of Assam. She experienced the trauma of patients first hand due to lack of proper medical infrastructure and took it upon herself to start 'Better Life,' a chain of affordable high-end medical facilities even in the last mile. As a medico-entrepreneur, Dr Bhattacharjee could successfully replicate the Better Life model and wishes to do more across India, so that another patient does not die in this 21st century due to lack of basic medical needs, be it medicine, or a simple operation or even a difficult delivery.

This book is not just inspiring, it is also a lesson to all about how a woman, single-handedly can fight against odds, against a system, and emerge successful in her mission with the least resources. All along she got the support of many, just like she faced hurdles too. Undaunted in her mission, she emerged a leader and shares her real-life story of setting up Better Life with her readers.

Pick up a copy! Get the inspiration to do something incredible!

Contents

Chapter 1

Landing in Udalguri

- 1 -

On the fringes of Udalguri, stands the blue Bhutan mountains looming large above the unending acres of tea gardens of Central Assam. A picture-perfect piece of heaven, that often hid the ugly heads of insurgency and appalling poverty gripping lives of locals. Nothing could or would change their misery, very few felt the need to uplift them from their deplorable sufferings specially when they fell ill. For hundreds of years, they kept doing what their forefathers did, working in the surrounding tea gardens, or doing odd jobs to earn a living. They kept suffering when sick, leaving their fate in the hands of the Almighty. Modern medical science had little hope to flourish in this remote area where mostly people had no access to basic medical services. Some had to travel hundreds of miles to the nearest big city of Guwahati during an emergency. They mostly met the inevitable fate en route—death!

Well, I was not born in this region, nor was I raised in Assam. But I simply fell in love with the picturesque green world around, the lilting birdsongs and the 'people' out here. They were simpletons by heart, honest and loyal, yet exploited. When I first landed in Paneri of Udalguri as a doctor of a well-known tea garden, little did I imagine, this would be the place from where my life's trajectory would change one day. My forever dream of becoming an entrepreneur would take its seed right on this soil. The journey was incredible, yet difficult.

Challenges have always made me stronger since childhood. The rebellious resilience silently nurtured by me, helped me create one of the most affordable medical services chains in one of the remotest parts of India.

Locals of Paneri were a mixed group, with tribes like Bodo, Rabha dominating along with Assamese, Bengalis, Oriyas and many others from different states of India who had come to work in the gardens. But they were bound by the same fate, poor medical service, so much so that even in the 21st century, pregnant women died during childbirth! When I landed as a doctor and visualised the pathetic scene, I made a conscious choice. I had to do something for these hapless people. I had always wished to bring a difference as a doctor, even when I was studying medicine in Kolkata. Finally, the stars aligned. And I got the opportunity to serve.

Bounded by Bhutan and Arunachal Pradesh and bordering Sonitpur and Darang, Udalguri was once part of the infamous Bodoland Territorial Region. The mainstay of local earning are the tea gardens. It was the only economy that thrived in the region since the British era when the colonial rulers brought tea leaves to the hills of Assam. I landed in Paneri on a splendid monsoon morning, travelling more than a hundred kilometers from the nearest city of Guwahati. The clouds seemed to be weeping, it was raining cats and dogs. Nature too seemed apprehensive of the fate of a city doctor in the middle of a Godforsaken land. My move raised many eyebrows back in my hometown. Many were clueless as to why I gave up a plush job in a Kolkata hospital and landed in such a remote location.

In 2015, I travelled all the way to Darjeeling Hills to join a tea garden, giving up my city hospital job. The gardens belonged to a well-known Indian multinational and I would be the garden doctor in charge of the tea-garden hospital. But my life changed for sure when after 2 years or so in 2017, I was transferred from the lovely upmarket gardens of Darjeeling where locals were much prosperous to the remote Assam tea belt where poverty and lack of basic facilities stared bare along with a language barrier. It was definitely a difficult change, but I went full on to face the challenge.

Many warned me: "Do not go, it is an insurgency belt. You are a single woman, think of your safety." Warnings however make me more of a daredevil. In this case too it had a different impact. I chose to ignore the warnings and follow my heart. It was a sort of 'soul calling.' The rebel in me popped its head and encouraged me to explore this new place. I left behind a wonderful city life with all amenities, to live in the dark deep jungles of a solitary doctor's bungalow. I drowned myself into hard work and pledged I would seek the best for the people around. That at times meant fighting with the authorities and the possibility of losing the job too! I stood steadfast. If Kolkata and Delhi educated me, Assam gave me life's biggest lesson, where I could use my specialisation in Gynaecology & Obstetrics and even my MBA degree in Hospital Management to full use. I realised I could finally use my basic skills as a doctor to save lives in Paneri, instead of carelessly referring them to Guwahati and shrugging off the responsibility. Most doctors around did that, even for a mildly sick patient and most patients died while travelling to Guwahati.

- 2 -

I was provided a huge doctor's bungalow. Though spacious, it was quite dilapidated, reminding one of its lost glory! And imagine the shock I got when I realised it stood right in the middle of an elephant corridor, at one end of the huge tea garden. The thrill however excited me and I was enjoying every challenge. Often after midnight I had to go on urgent calls to the tea garden hospital through that elephant corridor when usually pachyderms descended on the roads in herds. I was given a battery of servants and a driver. Seven people serving to be precise and that too for a junior doctor. My driver Nikhil Barman would say: "Madam, why don't you say no to these emergency calls at night. You can travel in the morning, why take the risk of encountering an elephant herd?"

My call was to help the patient, so I would confidently tell Nikhil: "Do not worry. You travel fast, it is an emergency, the woman is in labour." For me the patient's life was a priority.

Nikhil would still grumble: "Why Dr Parthajyoti never goes at night. He is not even available mostly during the day, either he is partying or goes on a long drive."

I knew Nikhil was concerned for my and his own safety, and what he was saying about my senior Dr Pathajyoti was true. The locals were used to such 'missing doctor' dispensary, often turned down. But how could I shun the duties that I was assigned to and sleep comfortably while a pregnant woman bleeds to death? Or just refer a critical patient without even trying to save him or her, perfectly knowing if I allowed the person to travel, they would die on the road. I would turn a deaf ear to Nikhil's warnings and journey to the hospital, wake till late hours, and stabilise the patient. Many such incidents happened and seeing me work diligently, even some of the nurses and ward boys felt motivated. In Assam, the maternal mortality rate or 'MMR' was one of the highest in India back then. The tea garden hospitals though had a big building, staring down as an imposing edifice in the middle of nowhere, the medical infrastructure was archaic. No new equipment, no proper medicines or vials of injections, and even life-saving drugs were mostly absent.

One day I asked my pharmacist Anup Ray, a Bengali raised in Assam: "Anup, why is there no Oxytocin injection? Isn't it a basic requirement for delivery? It is needed to stop post-partum haemorrhage." I had observed on some occasions that this basic injection needed after any delivery often went missing.

He replied nonchalantly: "That's because of cost cutting Ma'am. We do not have a proper refrigerator to stock the injections!"

I, being a newcomer, had little knowledge of this cost cutting trick. Anup added: "The more you refer cases to the hospitals in Guwahati, you can keep the hospital running cost low. Labourers and their families or locals who come to our hospital do not have any medical insurance or can afford Guwahati hospitals. Here they get free treatment, but we do not have any amenities or medicines that those hospitals can provide. Out of desperation the patients thus travel all the way to Guwahati, spending from their pockets, taking loans and we can save the treatment cost." So, this model gave me another shock wave. Cost cutting!

"And what about the government hospital nearby? Does it have any better facility," I asked.

"No, it doesn't. It is a 30-bedded civil hospital with tertiary care, but most of the time you will not find doctors or medicines or test machines. To the owners of any tea garden, the garden hospital is a liability, they have to give free treatment to the patients as per the Factories Act and hence we just do the basic minimum." Well I was enlightened and finally realised why tea garden hospitals were usually always in the middle of an archaic medical cycle unable to provide anything.

So, I decided to complain to my senior medical superintendent thinking he might help. I spoke about the lack of life-saving drugs, urging him to stock some. To my horror, he smiled and rejected my list of requirements point blank! Dr Parthajyoti in a superior tone advised: "Do not try to get into the administrative part. I look into it, you just treat the patients with whatever available in the dispensary and pharmacy. Rest you can refer to the city government hospital. Why bother?"

I replied calmly: "Ok, let me talk to the tea garden manager, if he can ask for additional funds." I was not to be perturbed, the unputdownable attitude of mine flickered.

Pat came Dr Parthajyoti's warning: "Going to the tea garden manager will not help." And he gave me a mocking smile.

Still, I went to the manager. He was a middle-aged Assamese man who had the power to refer to the head office anything he required. He could even change a doctor's posting. Unfortunately, I developed an extreme frictional relationship with him, because I was trying to bring about infrastructural changes in the hospital which did not go down well. He saw it as a negative challenge and started harassing me. He soon realised I was in the way of his cost-cutting measures. The manager wanted to gain some brownie points through the cost cutting programme, so that he would himself get a pay and post hike. But I wanted what was best for the patients, and their unnecessary sufferings due to lack of basic medical facilities pained me a lot. I was hell bent to do something for them.

One night sitting alone with a pregnant lady in labour, I realised there were deep gaps in the system and I needed to help. The patients too by then realised I was their dedicated doctor messiah unlike my predecessors. They developed a trust in me. Not just the tea garden employees and their families, even locals travelled for miles to be treated. News spread far and wide that I was always available at the hospital unlike others and successfully delivered difficult cases from breech to twin pregnancies. Locals had very bad experiences in the past and I suddenly became their beacon of hope.

During my free time beyond hospital duty, I went around the tea gardens creating awareness drives among the planters, teaching them about health and hygiene. In those remote areas, such awareness drives were badly needed. I tried to train the ward girls who were mostly locals and had little medical knowledge or expertise. I realised I would have to rewrite the system. It started with ordering proper branded medicines for the dispensary, much to the ire of my medical super. Nurses and ward girls helped me in my endeavour. They realised I was there to do good for them. During a difficult twin pregnancy, something unheard of at our hospital, the whole team stood by me throughout the night. That's the respect and loyalty you gain through honesty and dedication.

The pregnancy was a challenge indeed, particularly without any modern equipment. Jaya, the head nurse at first was sceptical about the twin delivery: "Doctor maam, tell the father that twin deliveries never happen in this hospital and this is a high-risk case. Send them to Guwahati. What if the babies die? We just have a labour bed and an obsolete baby warmer."

I was also a bit worried as there were no NICU facilities. I spoke to the woman's husband. Surprisingly he and his wife had so much faith in me, that they said: "You have been looking after the mother and babies since conception. Whatever happens, happens here!"

Their confidence in me multiplied the expectations that patients had in me and I decided to try my best. As luck would have it, one baby girl was delivered, the other refused to come out. The hospital had no caesarean facilities in hand and I had to normally deliver the second child with my hands, come what may! I stayed awake the whole night and finally the second baby was also delivered; both were girls, severely underweight. I wrapped the babies in cotton pads, as they were so tiny. Jaya and the other nurses, perfectly understanding what a feat I pulled through, cried in joy: "This hospital has created history, maam. The first twin delivery and that too the babies are alive."

I too swelled in pride, though I knew I had done the inevitable doctor's job and I was no God. Yet seeing the smile on the parents' face and holding the premature babies alive, I was so happy. I referred the babies to a neo-natal ICU and myself put them in the ambulance. Since then, local patients and tea garden families started treating me as their leader. I became one of them. They no more saw me as just a doctor, but as someone who stood by them in their hour of need. News spreads fast in the tea gardens. The whole community stood by me. On the night of the twin delivery, a local shop even opened its shutters past midnight to provide food for us. Our ward boy Bijoy asked: "Maam we all are hungry, I'm sure you are too."

I had literally forgotten what hunger was, as I was so deeply involved in trying to deliver the second baby healthy and keep the mother in a good physical state. But Bijoy's query made me realise I was hungry too. "But now it's past midnight, where will you get food from?" Bijoy reassured me and a local tea shop owner who got to know how I was saving twins and their mother, went out of his way to provide us biscuits and tea. The whole team was awake with me, as history was being created. They wanted to be part of that glorious moment. They all supported me in doing the 1st ever twin delivery in that hospital with meagre amenities.

- 3 -

Their love was so intriguing that in the very first year they invited me as a special guest to the Christmas celebrations at the local church. Most employees in the tea garden were Christians and the celebrations went on till the wee hours of the morning. The respect that these people gave me in their own simple ways was anytime better than a fat pay cheque of a city hospital. It reminded me of my early days as a doctor in a rural hospital of Sundarbans. Just after my medical school, I took up a doctor's job with an NGO in the Sundarbans. I always wished to serve in the villages, for that's where medical services are needed the most. Way back in 2006, the Sundarbans rural hospital opened a new vista for me where I had to do literally everything from A-Z. I performed multi-speciality cases, working on newborns to a

100-year-old, from administration to treating patients, doing OPDs, operations, awareness drives in boats and so on. This wholesome experience of Sundarbans in a way helped me in my versatile role as a doctor in Assam.

The respect of the locals was so deep that when the tea garden manager tried to transfer me to another garden as he took me as his enemy, all labourers called a one-day strike against the decision. They came together, blocked the way from my bungalow and though my belongings were on the truck as I had to move to a different location, they did not allow me to go. The manager had to revoke my transfer. Such incidents were unheard of, specially for an outsider, a Bengali doctor who had come as the plantation medic. But their support proved again that if you do your job with honesty and hard work, you will be befittingly rewarded in some form or the other. Over two and a half years that I worked in that garden, we all turned into a family. Even my house helps were mostly locals and they invited me with great pomp to their Bihu festivals. I was made the chief guest in multiple programmes. I was overwhelmed with their warmth and hospitality, their innumerable 'pithaa' treats during Bihu, and their songs and dances. Seeping in a new tradition and culture came automatically to me. It enriched me too. My explorer heart got food for thought.

I was so involved with my patients and staff that one day I saved a hospital pharmacist from his suicidal attempt. He was a middle aged local with a son. He tried to commit suicide by having sleeping pills due to some family feud. I could save him thankfully and that act was greatly appreciated by his family and neighbours. The locals became more confident in me.It so happened that a worker named Bihu had once drunk pesticide by stealing a bottle from the tea estate factory. He was in a critical shape and in the middle of the night he was being referred to a Guwahati hospital when a team of workers reached my quarters, woke me from my sleep and asked for help. I accompanied them to the tea estate hospital only to find Bihu in a critical state and the manager was constantly pressurising me to refer him, in case he died. I knew he would anyway die if he had to travel that long distance to any city hospital at night, so I decided to give it a try. The amount of pesticide he drunk was so much that it took atleast 3-4 saline washes using a Ryle's tube to save him. I could save Bihu and that came as a big relief to me for sure!

But the success was not easy. The journey was tough and tumultuous. My first encounter was with the labour union chief Sachindra Nath. He was a notorious leader in the area and everyone avoided him in fear. One day he brought his wife for a check-up. He said roughly: "Madam, don't refer her anywhere like other doctors did, you better treat her here itself."

I smiled at him and said: "Why should I refer?"

He then went on to lecture me: "Your predecessors always did that, you doctors are all the same. You are hand in glove with the managers and you exploit us."

I understood where the anger came from and rightfully so. It had deep roots in the mistrust between labourers and the management. But that very Sachindra after a few months came over and with folded hands said: "Madam, will you please come as a chief guest to our LP school? Our children will feel motivated by your presence."

I realised that day, winning hearts was not a difficult task. You just need to do your duties correctly. I was no more an outsider in the middle of those simpletons of the Assam tea gardens. They were with me in many of my initiatives and awareness drives, aimed at their future health. Most villagers in that area had genetic disorders like blood related thalassaemia and sickle cell disease. Regular screening for such diseases is a far cry in these remote areas and often these hereditary diseases attack them unknowingly. If a patient comes and says they are feeling weak, doctors think it is malnutrition. In reality, it is low haemoglobin arising from some genetic blood disorder. For such diseases constant blood transfusion is needed and I realised regular blood donation camps were a necessity in the area. I thus organised the first ever blood donation camp in the tea garden. The labourer families and many locals joined and contributed largely to my initiatives. They realised whatever was being done, was done for their good. I successfully mobilised the hospital team, the locals through awareness drives, something that was never done before. The locals were so touched that they wanted me never to leave.

However, the organisational politics was too much for me to handle and I resigned. By then I had already got the offer of Medical Superintendent at one of the largest mother and child hospitals of Guwahati. It was a very emotional good-bye and locals were so attached to me, they refused to let me go. Though I left in 2019 and went to Guwahati, I did regular medical camps and OPDs by travelling all the way from Guwahati to Paneri on every Sunday of the week. That was the level of attachment I had with the place. This was unheard of as the usual perception was in any North-East state outsiders were never welcome. And here was me, who these people were not ready to part with!

The Solitary Doctor's bungalow in Udalguri

The Blue Mountains of Udalguri

Celebrations with the Tea garden hospital team

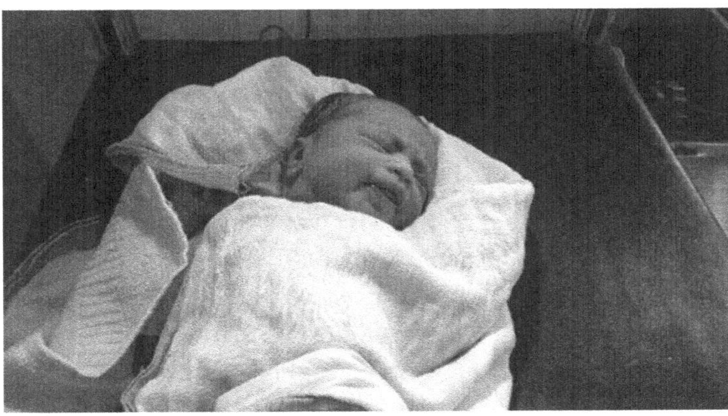

One of the twin babies that was delivered at the tea garden hospital

Chapter 2

Memories Shape the Future

- 1 -

It might seem unbelievable now, but I never wanted to become a doctor. I was always drawn to the idea of setting up something new from scratch, what we today call as Start-Ups. That ecosystem of being an entrepreneur was not so popular in those days. Let alone in a middle-class Bengali family, where becoming an engineer or a doctor was the be all and end all of life. My dad was no exception. Since childhood he had declared his diktat – "My two daughters will become doctors and doctors only!" Me and my sister were neither asked about our future ambitions nor were given a scope to think otherwise. I particularly was so terrified of my father's anger and mood swings that I accepted my fate and never questioned. But something uncanny boiled within me. Even if defiance at that stage was not possible, I turned into a silent rebel. I knew one day I will come out of this diktat and choose my own path.

My childhood was marked by two very important milestones. They left an everlasting influence on my future career path. Brought up in a nuclear family with a mother, father and a younger sister, four years junior to me, I was the typical elder sibling of the family on whose shoulders stood the weight of parental expectations. Above that with a father who was mostly missing on job trips or whenever home reflected anger issues, life was never smooth. The lack of freedom of thoughts in the face of my father's pressure only to follow what he said further led me to feel utterly insecure. My sister however was spared the rod mostly as she was younger and she wished to become a doctor anyway. Somehow her wishes and my father's diktat matched. It was a disaster in my case though. The negative impact it had on me was immense. As a growing teenager, I tried to overcome that by questioning everything that I was asked to do. I rebelled. A trait that was carried forward later in my work life, possibly in a positive way.

My mother was a school teacher, while my father, who came from a very humble background, was a self-made man. He worked with one of the largest MNCs of India. What could have been a happy middle class urban family with two kids, unfortunately turned into a difficult household. I often found it hard to cope. Surprisingly my educated and emancipated mother tolerated my dad's anger issues and tried adding a dash of normalcy in the family. She never protested. That further agitated me, as I wanted to speak freely. I was always put down. My father's wishes were final. We had no say in any matter. If I ever complained to my mother, her standard reply was: "I tolerate everything for you and your sister. These are parts of family life. And your father wants good for you both. Why not fulfill his dreams?" Anger seethed within me. I kept quiet though. But acceptance of such a behaviour was a far cry. Yet I toed the line of my father's wishes. Probably I thought that would bring peace.

Till Class V, I was raised in Kolkata. A very haunting memory of those years was locking myself in the bathroom every evening when my father returned home. The very sound of his car horn made me run to the bathroom and stay there for a long time, till my father settled in front of his television. But this had a positive side too. Since then, I developed an uncanny habit of doing things alone, taking risks, exploring new avenues. Every lesson taught me resilience, that somehow helped me float through with my future ventures. If I had a smooth life, I wonder if I could be the doc-entrepreneur that I am today, into multiple ventures, touching upon human lives. I started turning every negativity at home into positive achievements.

After Class V, we moved to Delhi. My dad was transferred to a senior position and was mostly missing from our daily lives. He used to travel a lot for work. Delhi was a complete change of scene from Kolkata. I really enjoyed the International School where we were admitted. It was a co-ed school, it offered several facilities from co-curricular to foreign language studies and so on that we did not get in the Kolkata school. I made full use of these opportunities that the school offered.

I took up the Japanese language. While most of my classmates were taking up French and Spanish, I went for a language that hardly anyone took. It was also a difficult language and the only language that had a different script. Looking back, I realise, I always loved difficulties. There were Indo-Japanese collaborations in those days and I took keen interest in the same, along with higher education facilities that Japan was offering. I studied Japanese for three years. I topped the class. Delhi being the capital, I met so many children from different states and countries. Interacting with a plethora of diverse people helped to boost my confidence, something I was lacking in Kolkata. The confidence unfurled even on stage, thanks to my teachers who let us participate in drama, debates and a whole lot of other activities. I had a huge stage fright, but thanks to Mrs Bina Suri, who was also my class teacher and others, I participated in annual day functions and did things I was shy of earlier. There were competitions where I had to speak on stage. The culture of thinking, innovating and bringing the thoughts on the table helped me later in life in my entrepreneurial venture. Something I was not encouraged at home, I was allowed in school. A lot of celebrities came to our annual day function at the famous Siri Fort auditorium of Delhi. We sisters participated in front of so many dignitaries. Then there was the Scholars Award. Every year whoever topped the class or got beyond 90 percent received the Scholars Award. They were made to stand on stage with a different coloured batch and different blazer. Every year I got that Scholar's Award and standing on the stage with other toppers inculcated within me a sense of security and pride. That I can do it!

- 2 -

In Delhi, the household was primarily centred around my mother, in our father's absence. I heaved a sigh of relief to some extent. Mom took good care of our emotional needs, from our education to taking us out for movies. Me and my sister were never allowed to go out with friends. The environment in Delhi social circles was very different from what we had in Kolkata. The society was open, hip and happening. People mingled very freely without much parental interference. The liberal society was a big transformation for me and we lived in South Delhi, a very posh locality. Young girls and boys went out on dates, to night clubs, to movies, partying around. While we only had to study and be the class toppers. I had no other choice. We were not even allowed to go on trips or excursions. My classmates often made fun of me for leading such a severely disciplined life. They would ostracise and tease me: "There goes the walking talking encyclopaedia. She only studies all day and night." This was followed by wild giggles and laughter.

When father was home, there was always a strict code of conduct. No parties, no hanging out with friends after school. Dad said clearly: "The car will pick you after school is over and you will return home asap. Same rule for tuition classes." When it came to annual report card day, another drama would unfurl at home. I always questioned the '*parampara*' of showing the report card to my father. "Ma why should we need to show it to dad?

You teach us. You should be credited for raising two consistent class toppers."

Yet every year when our reports came, Ma said: "Go and show the report card to your father. Just rush to the sitting room, your father is reading a newspaper there. He will sign your report cards." Again, an act I was dictated to do against my wishes. But Ma was insistent. So with frightened steps, we sisters would finally reach dad's room and hold out our report cards to our father. Like the archaic head of the family, he would reply in a serious tone: "Oh ok, good, next time do better." And remember I stood 1st in class.

There was no praise, no hugging, no sign of being happy at a child's success. This made me realise that to my father "Nothing was enough." Not even being a class topper. And quite obviously the pride of being a class topper after a year's hard work would decimate in a flicker. After class X came another bombshell. I had filled up the form for commerce stream in my Plus 2, for that was my wish. My Ma had of course warned me against doing so. I did not listen, the subtle act of defiance however cost me heavily. My father scolded and tore the form and said: "Your only option is to become a doctor. I myself wanted to be, but never could. You have to be one."

So my future was laid as per my father's wish. A commerce degree would have helped me become the entrepreneur that I always wished to be. But I was not allowed to follow my heart. That's exactly what I am doing now. Despite being a doctor, I ventured to be an entrepreneur medic, to make lives better through the model of 'Better Life'. For 21 years I fulfilled my father's wish by working as a doctor. I was a good student and cleared every examination with a lot of success. That came automatically to me, like a robot programmed to act. I still remember on the day of my medical entrance exams I was literally in tears. Not because I had the apprehension that I might not clear the exams, but because I did not want to be a doctor. As usual, I came out with flying colours. I got admission in a leading medical college of Kolkata. But once I became a doctor, I took the opportunity to serve people. I decided to give it my best shot. I never concentrated on earning money, I decided to use my skills to serve humanity.

I refused to stick to the usual medico practice of starting off with city corporate hospitals. I wanted to serve in rural areas, serve the downtrodden who do not get the facility of good medical services. Thus my dreams took me to remote areas of Sundarbans. I then landed with 'Durbar,' the organisation working for the Sonagachhi prostitutes, finally I joined the tea gardens. At times I ask myself: "Was it my escape route from my family? To be away to remote locations? Or was it because of the true calling that I harboured since childhood?"

Then came a sudden shock when I was just 12 years old and was studying in Class VII. My mother was suddenly diagnosed with breast cancer. I overheard one morning a conversation between my parents about she having some chest pain for which she visited a local gynaecologist and realised she had breast cancer. I was so taken aback at the news, that I locked myself in the bathroom and cried. I made sure Ma doesn't see me crying, though I was scared from within. I tried to be a strong girl. In those days conservative surgery took place and her whole breast was cut off and she was in severe pain. She was in hospital for a long time and me and my sister used to visit her. When she returned home finally, she was asked not to go near the fire.

So, I picked up cooking and Ma used to instruct me sitting outside the kitchen, on a chair. That is how I learnt cooking and within a few days I was so grown up, taking care of my parents, my sister, packing our tiffin boxes and so on. I also witnessed my mother go through different phases of chemotherapy, how she lost her hair, and how she cried like a baby. But something that influenced me was her courage despite the nausea and fever after every chemotherapy session, she made an effort to get up from the bed the next morning and be with us. She did her job despite all the ramifications of cancer. She was thus a prominent example of resilience and how a cancer patient can bounce back. Later, she had relapses, for a long period, though she is fine now. But this entire journey of living with a cancer patient at home has been one of the earliest lessons I learnt as a child and that memory remains in my mind. That gives me a lot of courage even during bad times, I tell myself if Ma could do, I can also.

- 3 -

I was enjoying every risk I took to serve, far away from my dad's ambitions. I was now a doctor as per his wish, but what I would do as a doctor was my wish. I always had a business acumen and to hone up such skills, I joined pharma companies in sales and marketing. I scripted new business avenues. Then went on to do my MBA in Healthcare Management. By 2010, I was offered lucrative administrative positions in leading city hospitals. That stable and privileged life however did not go down well with my risk-taking appetite. I chose to land up in the tea gardens of Assam. I needed a wholesome role as a doctor that gave me the versatility of work and challenge of working somewhere remote. The immense excitement I got by bringing a difference in the lives of hundreds who were otherwise missing on the facilities that they deserve cannot be spoken in words. This hunger for crafting a new medical service ecosystem at par with urban facilities was continuously taking shape in my mind. I wanted to leave the comforts of home or a hometown and work alone in the middle of those who needed a doctor. I was also not up for any settled relationship in my personal life. Only my work kept me alive.

In 2015, going to the tea gardens of Assam was indeed a turning point of my life. Before I left Kolkata, between 2010-

2014, I was even running a pet shop on my own, my first business venture that was very close to my heart. None in the family supported this venture and my mother too was against it. But the seeds of entrepreneurship had germinated by then. There was no looking back. In every lecture or interview I give I say: "Entrepreneurship is about taking the road less travelled. It's about carving a space for yourself, by doing something that you are passionate about and on your own terms. Entrepreneurship, for me, opened a window to the world that I always wanted to create. It has helped me challenge myself, and in bringing out the best in me."

As a healthcare professional, I realised rural healthcare in many parts of our country needs to see change and a private-public model to enhance its scope. During COVID-19 in India, the urban healthcare infrastructures received a lot of attention and support from various avenues but their rural counterparts

suffered the most. COVID scare wasn't the only pin on the coffin. Rural healthcare system was jeopardized due to absence of doctors and paramedical personnel in rural hospitals. Even routine cases including pregnant mothers and children were left untreated. Lockdown meant people couldn't travel to cities for treatment as there were no transports available. Many lost their lives just because no vehicle could be arranged to take them to a hospital. And that's when my dream took the final shape. From the embers of a Pandemic was scripted my entrepreneurial journey.

Chapter 3

Setting up 'Better Life'

- 1 -

At the Guwahati Hospital, life was mundane, devoid of challenges I faced in Paneri. It was more like the run of the mill work as a medical superintendent with little freedom of bringing about changes. I always wished to be the changemaker. And I loved challenges. I was somehow missing the adrenaline rush. The hunger was not satiated as the owners who were also doctors had their own views. Meanwhile, news came from Paneri that shattered my heart. News of a 21-year-old pregnant woman dying during childbirth. I sat in my chamber alone after hearing this news. I told myself, I had to do something. This cannot go on. I had to stop these deaths which was easily achievable, only if these people got the right healthcare facilities at the right time. I was already in touch with the people of the tea gardens through medical camps that I conducted in these remote areas on and off.

It was also COVID times when doctors were hardly available. I made it a point to travel all the way from Guwahati to Paneri. Being a doctor, I was never stopped on my travel route. But the death of a young mother while delivering in the 21st century made me sit back and take a new course. Where is the flaw in the system? I asked myself. It was such a let-down for any doctor to lose people to situations that can easily be handled medically. I converted this loss that shook my entire being, into a new journey. I promised to myself that never again would another mother die due to lack of basic amenities. Not again will a child turn motherless at birth. It was indeed a defining moment, when I took up the risky challenge of starting my own venture "Better Life – Healthcare at the Last Mile." I set it as a for-profit, primary healthcare driven medical centre that included a multi-speciality family clinic, diagnostic centre, day care and pharmacy. The aim was to provide affordable, accessible, convenient, sustainable and quality-driven primary healthcare services to all, even at the last mile. My dream of being an entrepreneur finally took shape and that too in the service of mankind.

I knew how rural people were in dire medical distress in India. In Paneri they depended on me and with every knowledge as a doctor, I ran a literally one-woman show to give them the services. That meaningful dedication somewhat inspired me, which a corporate urban Guwahati Hospital could not. I was somehow losing the goal of my life. My out-of-the-box thoughts probably came from the lessons learnt from certain incidents since my childhood. I started questioning anything that I was asked to accept, either as a social custom or a family diktat. This time, I questioned the medical facilities.

'Better Life' was quality-driven, yet extremely affordable and dependable. Imagine an Ultrasonography machine in a remote area, state-of-the-art ECG, which would give you reports in a minute and cost you just Rs 200 whereas any Guwahati hospital would charge nothing less than Rs 500! Unbelievable! Modern primary healthcare services were provided to all at the last mile. I built a dedicated team of not just doctors, but of nurses, pharmacists, lab technicians. In those remote locations, the best option was to hire the locals. But due to lack of skill development, they hardly knew how to hold a saline bottle. I had to train them. The biggest challenge however came while finding a property to start the Better Life Clinic in Paneri. Whoever I approached was not too keen to give any space on rent for they thought a clinic or hospital meant blood and disease around. They were probably frightened of germs. No property owner was ready to give us a place in that rural set up. It being Pandemic times, the challenge increased manifold.

- 2 -

Interestingly, Assam houses have a typical structure. They usually are one storeyed, and have walls with a thatched tin roof. Around such a house there is usually a courtyard. Getting pucca houses in such remote rural areas was a rarity. After almost two months of property searching, I finally struck a deal. Just on the road, I came across a Cooperative Society building which was not being used. It almost looked like a haunted house and was dilapidated. I could convince the secretary of the cooperative to give the place on rent. I said: "I want to start a healthcare facility and it will be a blessing to all." He was convinced and handed over the place to us. Certain local residents and patients I had in tea gardens from the time I was a doctor there also helped me.

The first Better Life centre thus started on 14th February 2021 with a team of 9 medical staff and me as the doctor. Just like house hunting, building a medical team in a remote location was another challenge. In such areas it is very difficult to get trained medical staff locally and no one but the locals could be hired. Who would be as mad as me to come all the way from the city to dedicate his or her life for rural medical services? But I needed a team. So I thought of a plan. I looked for people who had some training and had no job in the villages. Or someone who passed class 12 and had no skills. I taught them the basics of medical handling, some were already trained and were happy to join. Those who were not qualified, I had to train them from A to Z. On the inauguration date, the local politician came. He knew me from my Paneri tea estate days. He encouraged us a lot and promised to help. This was indeed a win-win situation for him and the area. He realised what a gamechanger Better Life would be in that remote location.

The place I rented was around 1000 sq ft. with white walls and a green thatched roof. This was a colour combination well known as a hospital in those areas. Hence I chose that shade so that people around knew that we had set up a medical facility. The house had around 4 rooms. I turned one into a pharmacy, one into a clinic, and the other two rooms had certain beds and a reception. A small laboratory was also erected for collecting samples. The fenced area around the house had a green grassland. We erected makeshift walls to create a few more rooms and allow some more beds. And an area where patients and their families could wait. It was a mind-blowing comprehensive OPD care model and I took it to the next level by introducing more than 25 services.

My life turned into a challenge busting machine. Every other day there was one hiccup or the other and I had to run around fixing everything. The biggest challenge was training my half- educated staff. Initially I did not get any local doctors. I did every medical work myself. Later, doctors from Guwahati were roped in and I got into tie ups. Some doctors came once a month or once every two weeks. The only person however available 24X7 was me. Just like that man who stood on the burning deck, I was running around my dream venture turning it into a success story. I was like the omnipresent GOD, always available. Literally breathing, eating, drinking, sleeping only one word: Better Life. I realised in the initial phase that roping in services at the last mile would require involvement of technology. Else it was not possible to give quality service. So I had to train my staff to accept technology. Many did not even know how to use a computer. The idea was to bring the quality of urban healthcare in the rural sector. There was no quality, no standardisation. Better Life was a mission to give somebody a better quality of life and an easy name to remember.

- 3 -

Even though the adrenaline rush kept me going and so did my dreams, I did realise I had taken the biggest risk of my life. Even strangers asked me: "Why did you choose a place like Paneri in this whole world, a small and remote place to start such a venture and that too taking bank loans and on your own hard-earned money?"

I had only one answer: "It was my soul calling. Better Life was my only driving factor every day." Every single day, a new challenge surfaced. These remote areas are climatically very volatile, they are flood prone. Incessant rainfall could anytime flood the area, a bit of storm could lead to power cuts for days. Above all there was the fear of COVID Pandemic that wreaked havoc even with the most sophisticated medical system of the world. To withstand power cuts I had to arrange for a generator. I had to run basic machines for my patients. Getting a generator in such a remote area itself was a challenge. One was finally located from a place 50 kms away and brought on a rainy and stormy night. It was a basic model and when fixed it created a whirring noise. Like waves of disaster, the generator worked, but the sound it created irked neighbours. They started complaining, especially at night. But the Better Life clinic was open 24x7, so we had to provide service. One night it so happened a patient was delivering, there was a power cut, the generator was on, and I had to rush from the delivery table to the peripheral fenced area as a group of neighbours were agitating against the sound that the generator created! A trouble shooter for sure and I had to cool their frayed nerves.

One stormy day, the makeshift shed made for patients to sit comfortably was blown away. I could not make a concrete structure as it was a rented property. At times there was no water, at times no power. Literally basic amenities were missing and here I was, a female doctor from Kolkata, running the show despite the challenges.

For two long years, it was just me. It was only 'Better Life' for me. I had no personal life. I became a local resident. That too was a big challenge, to get a place for me to stay. Most houses in the area were temporary or kutcha houses. The pucca houses had separate washrooms that were outside. This was no planters' bungalow that I got when I was with the tea estate. Someone informed me that a man was building a house nearby and had a small space still left infront. I ran there to request him to construct one room for me with an attached washroom and kitchen. In Assam type houses nobody could imagine having an attached bathroom. Thankfully he complied and finally I had a roof on my head.

As I said, challenges were unending. As technology use was my prime motto, you need a proper network for that. But over in Paneri internet connection was erratic. All my machine software ran on the internet. There were days when to send an email, or to attend a webinar, I had to sit in my car to find a place where I could get network and then connect. But I was almost in a trance, I had to make Better Life work and I did make it work. Within four years, from one centre, Better Life went on to five centres. My team of 9 jumped to 40 plus members. And my dream venture took off with a thumping victory!

The First Premise of Better Life

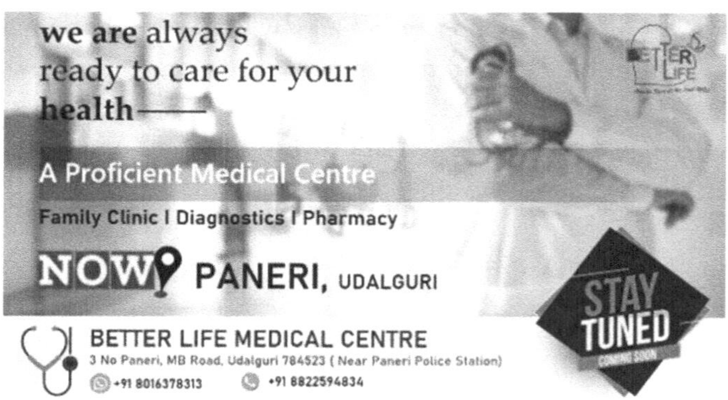

Our FIRST TEASER before the grand launch

Launch Day

Chapter 4

First Ever: USPs of Better Life

\- 1 -

Days and months seemed to come and go with me running from pole to pole to set up the infrastructure, the team and above all create awareness about Better Life. A month after inauguration, on 8th March 2021, on Women's Day we conducted the first ever free women's health camp in Paneri. Nothing of this kind had been seen before. Just for women! So long only men dominated in medical camps. But the drive was a humongous success, with 100 plus women of different ages participating.

In rural areas there are unique ways of creating awareness. We used a mic on a rickshaw, went from village by village, and in local language made people aware of our services. Involving local resources was my prime aim. I took the Asha workers into confidence. They were my best bet as 'loudspeakers for Better Life.' They had access to every home and on a whispering campaign they went around from door to door. Next we took help of village headmen and involved 50-60 villages around Paneri. In Assam, they are called Gaon Burra. A few of them were extremely helpful and went out of their way to help in awareness building and set up screening camps, bringing in locals. They played a very active role and spread the news of the services Better Life provided to others, so that we got cooperation from local villages.

In a first of its kind, we introduced patient pick up services, not only those who were sick, but even those who needed tests and could not come to our facility due to logistic issues. Our vehicles brought in pregnant women for USGs and again dropped them back home. This service was so unique that it was extremely appreciated by patients and their families. We were the first healthcare providers who used social media for creating awareness in the Assamese language, keeping local cultural practices in mind. We used videos, graphics etc leveraging social media in a rural set up. I involved the team to create content through videos and awareness designs.

- 2 -

Another first was introducing an eye care clinic where instant spectacles were made. The doctor would do the eye testing, give the power, and the specs were made then and there so that patients could take the spectacles at one go. This helped patients to save time and travel from remote areas as the solution to their eye power was taken care of right then.

Another concept that became very popular was 'special offers and special packages.' Though in urban cities and towns consumers always are pampered with multiple offers and choices, in a remote rural set up, it is unheard of. The offers brought in were very exciting for customers as well. For example, when we launched our new Health Supplement as per WHO guidelines, it was sold under the brand name BL Pro+ and was priced affordably. It had varieties for all ages, one was Pro+ Diabetic to manage Diabetes, one for the mother known as Pro+Momz as a complete nutrition for Pregnant and Lactating women, one for growing children known as Pro+ Kidzz and Pro+ Energy was for everyone designed to deliver high standard nutrition. We often gave offers like if one bought a jar of Pro+Momz , they would get a jar of Pro+ Kidzz for free. On special occasions such as Independence Day & Bihu, we gave discounts on all these supplements and that was hugely appreciated.

Some pharma companies also participated in our camps and distributed free ORS etc. A huge radius of 25-30 km was covered from one clinic. We used local journalists for press coverage and more people got to know of Better Life in the process. News spread fast and my dreams turned to reality. Reaching the last mile with superior medical knowhow was something I aspired to as a doctor. Finally that started taking a definite shape.

Our centre also did minor operations, delivery, abortions, dressing, plastering of fractured limbs. We did not have an OT, so major operations could not be performed. During COVID times we were the first movers, the only clinic with oxygen concentrators and pulse oximeters. We had COVID test kits, PPE kits etc which even government facilities around did not have. I managed to get them from Guwahati so that we could do the screening. We even introduced COVID immune packs with immune boosters, masks and hand sanitisers. We collaborated with nearby NGOs for making cloth masks, selling them at a very nominal price from the pharmacy. That gave employment to locals too. But I did not rest at that. I, with my team, did a lot of awareness activities, going around in villages, teaching the basics of handwashing with soap, a basic requirement to keep one safe during the Pandemic. In a place where even primary healthcare facilities were not available, where dispensaries closed down after noon, Better Life came as a blessing to many!

- 3 -

Today, Better Life has a model of unique services. We have included emergency medication, oxygen, medicine delivery, nebulisation. I brought in Tele ECG in such remote areas where no cardiologist was required on site. The ECG machine through software is linked to a centre in Bangalore where instantly a cardiologist sitting in Bangalore reads the graph and gives the report in minutes. Logistics issues were thus solved with the help of technology.

People of tea gardens and surroundings often suffer from Tuberculosis. We thus set up a TB Dot centre in collaboration with the state government. We were the only private healthcare facility who was authorised with the Dot centre, providing diagnosis, free medicines, and monitoring for TB patients. Patients no longer had to run to government hospitals where they mostly never got the required treatment on time. We even had Trop T test kits which look like a pregnancy kit, giving identification of whether a person with symptoms is having or is going to have a heart attack. A lot of people were saved because of these kits. We introduced Pap Smear tests for women and adult vaccinations like anti Cervical Cancer vaccines, anti snake venom injections, rabies vaccine etc. Though such vaccines are supposed to be stocked in government hospitals, mostly they are unavailable in primary healthcare centres. Many locals came to us for the vaccinations. People realised they were getting everything under one roof and that too quality medical services.

Like our nurses always wore gloves, something unthinkable in that rural area where hygiene was never given top priority. We did though like any other urban private health centre. Low-cost health supplements were introduced. The mission was to give whatever is required to create a healthy society. To give this sick population a quality healthcare service, where usually people had to run from pillar to post even for a simple paracetamol. Better Life was a magic box for them. People could not believe it at first that in that small place so many services were available and at such low cost. Asthma, COPD patients had to travel for nebulisation long distances and had to avail of costly services whereas we gave the same services, if not better, at a throwaway cost and that too 24x7. Same for diagnostic screenings like USG, ECG and so on. We were not just cost effective, we were always available for medical emergencies. We made baby warmers available and even photo-therapy services for neonatal jaundice cases available in such remote villages. Our doctors charged only Rs 100! But we never compromised with quality and dedication. That went on, in a sustainable mode.

Unfortunately, in India, rural healthcare is still under slumbers when compared to its urban counterpart. It is either left to the Government to arrange services or limited to the not-for-profit sector only. There are almost no private players in this sector in the rural front. Hence people still suffer from ailments that may be unheard in the city today. Basic healthcare facilities are often miniscule and lack quality standards. Thus, I was very clear right from the beginning that I wanted to create a difference here. At Better Life, we do not compromise on quality and make sure we have the latest machines and technology to cater to the best of healthcare. Yet we have worked ardently on the pricing such that it is affordable to the rural people and no one is denied treatment owing to lack of money. The clinics have the latest equipment, technology driven, to ensure faster and more accurate results that are absolutely crucial for correct treatment. They use telemedicine for a few services for expert help in remote areas. Technology also saves time and makes human resources more efficient and effective.

For a rural market, listening to a customer is equally easy and difficult. Often one needed to make an extra effort to reach the customer. Though s/he may not be educated, but still had opinions and pretty significant ones! So, the team invested in time, energy and resources. Better Life clinics had to compete with local quacks who took the people for a ride without providing modern medical services. To give that modern medical services, we held health camps, many times specifically for women. We provided women health checkup packages, injectable contraceptives, worked on patient nutrition with free diet charts, keeping a tab on chronic illnesses like Diabetes,

Hypertension, Kidney ailments etc. We spoke to them about foetal anomalies and how to give birth to healthy babies, what all a mother should eat and do. With Home collection and 24*7 emergency services, Better Life ensured even the remote rural population receive the same treatment as those living in top cities get even at night with a night pharmacy in place. We literally opened up a new vista in the Healthcare Sector.

For the incredible work that was being done here, Better Life was awarded at multiple events of which the following are notable –

- 'Champion of Cause' at the MSME Honors (East) 2023
- 'Best Woman Entrepreneur' at the Bengal Leadership Awards 2023
- 'Outstanding achievement in Health & Wellness' at the North East Women's Conclave 2023
- 40 Under 40 Passionate Women leaders in Healthcare 2023
- India Social Impact awards 2022
- Influential Women Leaders in Business 2022
- India's 100 under 40 by Fox story India
- The Real Superwoman Award 2022 by Forever Star India
- Entrepreneur of the Year 2021 (Healthcare)

Face masks handmade by the rural women of SADICHSA NGO during COVID times

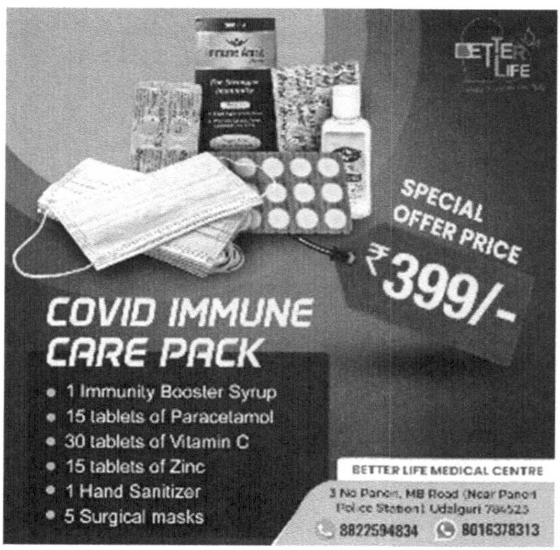

COVID Immune Packs designed and promoted by us were the first of its kind in Udalguri

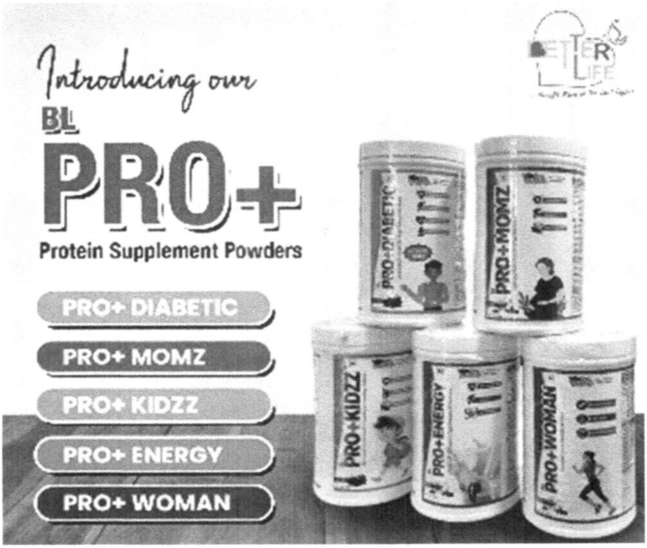

The launch of our own supplement range at Better Life

Receiving an award from the internationally acclaimed film maker Ms Rima Das

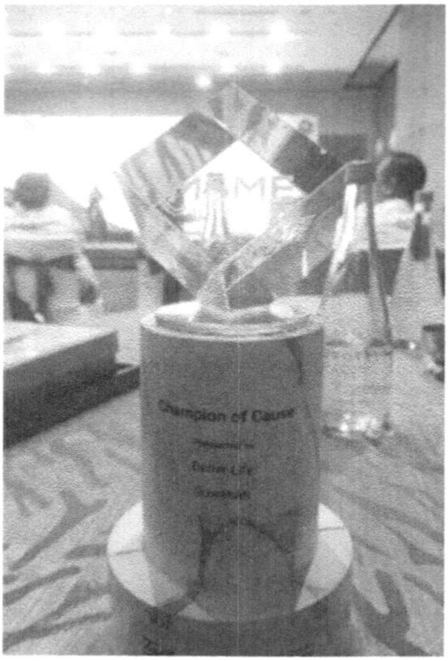

Champion of Cause Award

The Bengal Leadership Award

At the North East Women's Conclave Awards

Chapter 5

Strategies to Penetrate Last Mile

\- 1 -

Most women of my age would have dreamt of domestic bliss, having a family, doing a stable job. For me it was just the opposite, I dreamt always of creating something revolutionary, that would touch upon the lives of those who have for years been deprived of the basic medical amenities. It was an excruciatingly hard time, juggling between my medical services that I was giving to the patients hands on, being present 24x7 and managing the centre with my team, trying to reach out as much as possible to the last mile patients. However my smile and determination never faded. For what I was doing was something that I loved, it was my dream, the dream of being an entrepreneur, never to be bound by the shackles of a set job. I had ideas since my college days, ideas that would be changemakers if implemented in the right format and I was putting most of it to use. The journey was not a bed of roses, rather I faced more thorns than I ever imagined. It was a big struggle and though there were many who were warming up to our endeavours, there were again some who were making our work more difficult, posing threats and challenges along the way.

Looking back, it was like a storm before a calm. Before a constructive model is put in place and it starts functioning full on, an umpteen number of challenges float in. In my case the same happened. I faced it with my marketing and communication skills that I had picked up early in my career due to my work among varied people. I knew I was dealing with the 'people' factor. I could also put to use the theoretical knowledge I acquired during my MBA course. We had been taught marketing strategies, but now I realised I had a forum where I could really use them with my own set of interpretations and innovative technology. I had to be experimental as I had meagre resources that I had to use in that remote location. Every work in Better Life had to be seamless, as we were dealing with both very sick and not-so-sick individuals who needed different kinds of approaches. We were not just fighting disease and germs, but trying to keep up the human interaction quotient alive.

The basic lesson in marketing is always 'Identifying the Target Audience.' For me that was a tricky job as everybody seemed to be my target audience. Every household had one sick person around. No one in that whole region seemed to be in the pink of health. So I had no option in the beginning, I could not just target one particular segment, rather as a doctor I had to treat everyone.

But I soon realised that everyone cannot be my target audience. So it zeroed down to those people who were sick and also who wished to get cured. Am I sounding dichotomous? Well no. You might think every sick person wishes to be fit and fine. Here, that was not always the case. Being away from a corporate hospital, in a space where nothing was tapped in-depth ever before, I experimented with my vision as a doctor. I started speaking to locals about their ailments and disease and their views of being healthy. Interestingly, I realised since the British era, the majority of population in a tea garden and its surroundings are perennially sick. And why so? Because the British planters wanted them to be sick always and hence brought in unhealthy practices to which these people got so addicted that even today they have not been able to come out of it.

I shall give you a surprising example. In the tea gardens after lunch hours, liquor tea comes in big tankers for the workers. They open the taps and start having them in cups and this practice was brought in by the British for two reasons – the caffeine in tea kept the workers wide awake, so that they never felt tired after hours of standing and constantly plucking tea leaves. Also if one takes liquor tea after food, iron and folic acid of the food does not get absorbed due to the caffeine. As a result, most people in that area were anaemic and also addicted to tea. It was like a double target game – the people are always tired as they are anaemic and they do not even wish to get out of the tea garden. Currently many in the younger generation are now going out of this so-called comfort zone and getting educated, trying other jobs.

But for generations most of these people never wished to be cured, rather they chose to stay sick. That's a result of a mind game that was played for years on them by the British planters and later the various tea companies who owned the gardens.

- 2 -

So my target audience were people who wished to be cured. I questioned many to understand their thought process, at times picking up a casual conversation. Sadly I realised most of them had no concept for all these years about a life outside the tea gardens, they are born here and they feel they will die here, in between doing a job within the garden and earning a paltry sum.

At times even for a leave quota that the company gives them, they would feel contended. So they were in a way happily sick, to get the leave. Some even took the leave on grounds of sickness and went to Guwahati on a trip or do some other work to earn more beyond the tea garden duty. Most of these people are dependent on the tea garden authority who pays their medical expenses and they do not usually go elsewhere for treatment.

They are either sent to government hospitals or to the city medical colleges directly. They know the tea garden authority will give them everything – from basic treatment, to their child's education in tea garden schools, to even their funeral expenses. To them the tea garden is their heaven and they never explored the horizon beyond, even if they lacked the basic amenities and infrastructure and on several occasions were outrightly exploited. Yet their lives revolved around that place only, forever embedded in the deep dark pit of a vicious cycle.

My initial strategy was not to cater to this crowd, but to those who wanted affordable quality treatment at their doorstep, spending some amount of money for the services. We zeroed down to such a population. I used local resources to identify and mobilise them because I was an outsider, I needed insiders who the people would trust. We used Asha workers, Anganwadi workers, even local quack doctors, Gaon Burras, Bejiwalas for this purpose. Ah! The Bejiwalas were an interesting lot. They had access and acceptability in the local community, they were the ones who went around giving injections. I have no idea how they learnt the art of giving injections, maybe they picked up the expertise somehow and went on their bicycles from village to village giving injections. They were thus trusted by the villagers.

In the beginning we unfortunately found ourselves in a conflict zone with all these people. From local quacks to bejiwalas – everyone saw us as their competitors. As our popularity grew, patients who were going to quacks so long, were now coming to 'Better Life' and hence the practice of the quacks was going down. It was a direct hit to their interest. So the whole scenario ended up in conflict. I had to navigate through this war-like zone and come out successful. I started mapping a strategy thus. Instead of alienating them, I decided to take them into confidence and started inviting them to 'Better Life' for certain events like Health camps, training programmes etc. We opened a communication channel and even created a business module for them, giving them the importance they were vying for! They were now pleased.

We made a model of giving them cash rewards for referrals and services that they cannot give but could refer patients to us as we were equipped to give the same. Hence we created an environment where we were complimenting and not challenging their services. In two years, I successfully created a network of 100 plus people who went around marketing 'Better Life.' Gaon burras also started helping us in leadership roles. Like local Asha workers who did not listen to us, listened to these Gaon Burras. We started giving small doles to these people and involved educated local youths who were unemployed, and did not wish to go out of their village for any city job. We trained them to be a part of our system.

- 3 -

Our concept was thus to increase our visibility. In Assam even in villages student unions in local schools and colleges were important. They were also sometimes very helpful in mobilising people for camps. We asked them to help us too. We also launched some interesting programmes like 'Arogya Sparsh.' My team including nurses, pharmacists etc would visit home to home in villages. Many villagers initially had inhibitions coming to the doctor, might be due to language issues, superstition etc. So we went to the patients instead. The team was trained by me with certain basic health and hygiene courses, they went with blood pressure and sugar machines. We did it for almost a year. Nobody else before that had gone on home visits. Better Life provided such a service for the first time. Home visits were totally free of cost. This model proved to be a huge success.

Then we created 'Better Life Smart Points' at junction points, say 5km or beyond from the Better Life centres. We chose important shops and key local care centres and set up banners for our smart points. The idea was when patients wanted appointments and could not contact us over phone, they could go to these Smart Points and take an appointment for a particular day and service. Say on a Sunday, someone needed an USG, they could book in advance at the Smart Point. They were also used for medicine delivery to patients. The Smart Point owner got commission from us. It was giving business to us both and for the patient it was a known local point from where several services were available.

I even used influencer marketing so many years ago, when it was literally unheard of and that too in such a remote location. Local influencers spoke in the local language. We chose the ones who were very active on social media, mostly facebook people, some people who everyone listens to, may be political or apolitical, for particular villages. We identified such people and many of them were our patients. Then local media also in Assamese language, you tube news channels carried our news. Social media was used by us bigtime and my employees even made content, made podcasts, someone else dubbed my medical advice in their local accent and passed it on to a huge audience through social media.

Amidst all these efforts, the gamechanger was recording testimonials of happy patients. They helped in talking about us and our superior services. Needless to say these villagers felt like VIPs giving bytes and were very proud to spread the news about us. Through word of mouth our patients brought other patients. Everyone in my team were locals, I did not even bring anyone from Guwahati or from any other region. I picked up local people, who were not even tech savvy. Better Life made their lives better too through job generation for locals.

- 4 -

But everything was not hunky dory. There was a local government dispensary right beside Better Life, and officials there were troublesome. The government doctor there was creating trouble, he shut down the dispensary at 1pm, and was trying to sabotage us, spreading rumours. By then we had already 12k plus registered patients. No one ever had such a big number, and they were getting help from our multi speciality services for all kinds of ailments. Local political goons were trying to utilise this opportunity to extract money. Udalguri already had a history of insurgency and though terrorists had surrendered, now they had turned into local musclemen. And they kept muscle flexing at the drop of a hat to extract money. Even local communities who were my beneficiaries, sometimes bad mouthed, saying we took money, instead of discussing how affordable we were! They thought everything was charity. There was a continuous flow of good things happening as well as challenges.

I had a particular way of communication, those who were not my well-wishers, I called them and spoke to them. I never shunned them. For a solution, I called these people who were trying to sabotage, specially those who were known to me. Some were even patients who we had saved. Very strange isn't it? They owed their life to us, yet they never praised our services. Maybe that's how the world runs, where the more you give, the least you get. But I always feel communication is the key to any solution, though local language was a barrier for me, yet I talked it out with everyone. If you have an intent of communication, you can do it, and it can solve half of the problems.

As for the local goons I had good relations with Paneri Police Station, which was beside Better Life. We started providing services to the policemen and the OC free of cost to keep ourselves in their good books. They usually helped us on many occasions and whenever we complained they took it seriously. Just because I was a woman, non Assamese, running a business, so I was always an easy target. In such cases we took help from local forces. There was not even a day when we did not have a challenge. In the initial few months the local quacks said what not to hold on to their patients. We had a competitor located 10 km away from us, a private clinic, running for 10 years, and the owner was a local tribal man. They did not have quality service and no night service. And since he was not a doctor like me, he could not give 24X7 medical services that I could give as I was always present. They tried to take away our patients, they would send people posing as patients doing videos, trying to take away our employees too. People, climate, local politics – everything came as a challenge. We had to show a person that business is separate and charity is separate. Charity cannot happen all the time, for me it was a sustainable model as I was giving quality service. The only thing villagers know of is a government hospital. So to register the concept of 'Better Life' where for quality healthcare one has to pay a minimum price was a big challenge. Setting this into the hearts and minds of locals was a humongous challenge. My marketing skills came as a blessing and that brought success for sure.

Penetrating the last mile with our AAROGYA SPARSH program

Penetrating the last mile with our AAROGYA SPARSH program

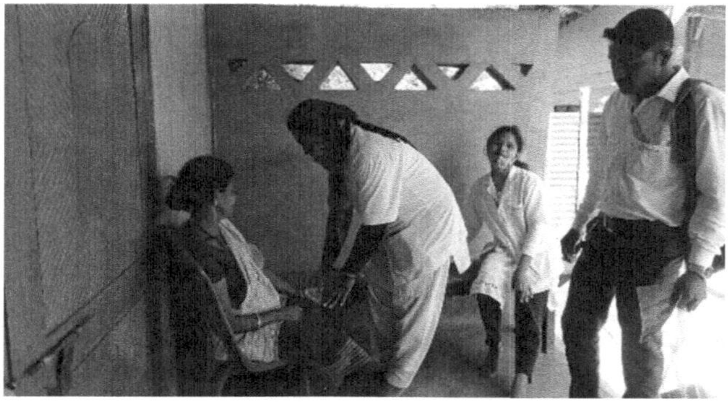

Chapter 6

Being an Inclusive Leader

- 1 -

I am often asked what is the secret to setting up a perfect harmonious organisation from scratch? Just like I did in the case of 'Better Life.' I tell my admirers: "There is not one ingredient to it, one needs to mix and match, one needs to experiment with models and human minds, to realise which model would finally succeed. When I started 'Better Life,' I was the captain of the ship that had just set sail. The waters it would encounter could be rough, or stormy, or even smooth. Who knows? I didn't for sure. But I knew I had to steer the ship well. I had to lead my team without creating or inventing any new mantra of leadership, but put to use those that I already knew. I had to focus on what I wanted and lead by example.

In my job life as an employee of different organisations of India, I had the luck of witnessing different kinds of leaders along my journey. I would not put them under roles of good, bad, ugly, rather I felt there were two types of leaders broadly – autocratic and democratic. Now which one would I be? I never wished to be an autocratic leader, even though 'Better Life' was my baby, my brainchild, without any help from anyone, either family or friends, it was run by just me and my vision. Still, I knew I did not possess it, if I had to be a good leader, I needed to dissociate myself from the concept that I was the supreme authority. Rather, I needed to blend with everyone and make them feel I was just another employee like them. To whip up a good dish, you need all the ingredients and spices given in the correct proportions, mixed in the right ratio, similarly to run a successful enterprise, a leader needs everyone to be part of the same dream.

I genuinely believed leadership is not just about giving instructions, but it is much more than that. So the democratic leadership style appealed to me and I pursued it throughout 'Better Life' and I do it even today. I feel the 'team' should always be a part of strategy making and if you can strike the right balance there, then the organisation will always succeed, else it will fail for sure.

To make the team feel they are valued and their opinions and suggestions are equally important to me, I started the concept of 'Monthly Meetings.' Though such meetings are common in an urban company, for rural people who do not even have prior job experience or for those who worked in small unsystematic organisations, monthly meetings are a new concept. So my team at 'Better Life' was very excited to be part of such structured meetings and they were equally honoured that they were called to the table to share their views too.

- 2 -

We started meeting on the 1st day of every month. I created an amiable environment at the meeting, no one should feel they are held at gunpoint and forced to listen to my lectures for hours and they keep quiet throughout. On the contrary, I divided the meeting schedule into two halves. In the 1st half, I would speak and tell them about what happened well in the organisation and what did not go so well in the past month and what improvements I expected them to make, to correct the issues. I would also share my future plans to make the team a part of the plan. In the process, I was showing and expecting a similar vision from the team, so that they would be encouraged to put in their own concepts, enriching my vision further.

It also sent a strong message to the team, needless to say a happy one, that I valued my team. I encouraged them to value-add to the suggestions I made, instead of simply brushing aside any ideas they thought could be implemented and just putting forward my views, forcing them down their system.

Because I was giving value to their suggestions, they felt important and accepted me with open arms. They valued me, I was no more an outsider to them. Even when I worked as a doctor at the tea gardens, I felt these people treat you as an outsider, till you can actually make yourself a part of them. And I knew how to make that, how to create one big family!

I was socio-economically richer than them, more educated than them — attributes that had every chance of acting against my inclusive plans. So I automatically built a bridge in the process, by making them a part of my vision and plans, making them feel they are as important to me as I am to them. They no longer said: *"Aap to baare admi hai, hum toh chhote admi hai."* I could bridge the gap successfully and that helped in the smooth sailing of 'Better Life.'

The monthly meetings became very good ice breakers and worked very well. The staff would eagerly wait for the 1st of every month to arrive, not for the salary, but for the meeting. They took it so seriously and sincerely, that they came ready, jotting down points, eagerly scripting suggestions. There were many lengthy discussions that were followed with sumptuous samosas and hot piping *chai.* Isn't it said the route to your heart is at times through good food? I ensured that delicious snacks were served at the meetings to keep the energy going.

In the 2nd half, every team member was invited to the pedestal and asked to speak — giving their suggestions, if any complaints they had, interpersonal issues they encountered, how to resolve that if any, how as a team we wanted to take 'Better

Life' ahead and so on. This exercise had a great impact otherwise also. It improved the communication skills of every member, and boosted their overall confidence, which was so low when they first started working with me. In a way such meetings benefitted all of us.

A lot of programmes we introduced in 'Better Life' were courtesy to these strategy meetings, and we tried to implement the suggestions that came out of these meetings. The democratic style of leadership for me, placing the team ahead of me, from day one, was a mantra that I tried to instill in all of them.

My mantra was clear and loud:

"Customer First/ Patient First.

"Team 2nd."

"Organisation 3rd."

And last was me!

- 3 -

This revolutionary hierarchy that I successfully established, made the team feel special. A lot of them became more proactive in their services and took active interest in whatever 'Better Life' was doing. New ideas were flowing in, multiple brainstorming sessions were held and then they came up to me. There was so much excitement and positive energy around!

I also taught my team how to counsel and initiate a conversation with a patient and how to get more referrals from our current patients. So in a way they were learning to handle customers and also creating the sales pitch. When some problem or challenge came, I left them to solve the same, to boost their confidence, but I also stood by them and we faced every pitfall together. That in a way made the bond stronger and there was no scope of any kind of blame game. Everyone was held accountable for anything, starting from me to the last mile employee.

They were no more mere employees going away with a salary. They needed to feel the organisation belonged to them too, just like it belonged to me. That sense of belonging and feeling responsible for any action, helped to create an environment where everyone had the other person's back. This work culture that I created was a kind of model that could be replicated in any organisation for seamless running of a place. I have seen many organisations that are mere chatters, displaying mantras on board but not putting them to work in real life. The mantras are not followed mostly. But if I could ingrain it in them as the culture of an organisation, then like the keys of a piano, they all play in unison.

The most important aim was bidding goodbye to class culture within an organisation, creating accountability, instilling an essence of togetherness and spirit of unity. I always said as a motivational call to all:

"If I fail, you also fail, if I succeed you do too."

We started with just 9 people and then grew to a 45 plus staff strength. I always believe 'Team building' is one of the most essential roles of a good leader and if a leader is not clear about his or her vision and culture one needs to make, then unfortunately, good teams will never be formed. Team building in a rural area, where no one had any clue about how corporate organisations work, was thus a responsibility as well as a challenge for me as a leader.

- 4 -

Like a sudden bolt from the blue, some incidents occur in your life that rock your whole foundation. Yet you need to tide over the storm and keep calm. But they always leave behind a big mark in your work life and you grapple to navigate through the confusion and loss that harp on the team. One such incident was the sudden loss of a very dear employee of 'Better Life,' Sumi.

Sumi was just 24 years of age when she joined as a receptionist at 'Better Life,' she was the youngest member of my team, bubbly and energetic. I loved her like my daughter. After a year of work, she suddenly died at 25, from a cerebral stroke, something that was unbelievable even for a seasoned doctor like me!

It was so sudden, that none of us were prepared to face the consequences. I still remember that day during annual Bihu celebrations. We also had a celebration at 'Better Life' the previous day. Sumi danced, she sang and we all had a gala time. The next day when she did not arrive on time for her duty, my staff called her up. This was very unlike Sumi, she was a very responsible girl.

She stayed in a nearby house as a paying guest. When my staff came and informed us that she neither arrived, nor was responding to calls, we decided to send someone to her place to check on her. The door had to be broken open and she was found unconscious, lying on the floor. Sumi was rushed to 'Better Life' and I examined her and realised she had a cerebral stroke. We gave her emergency medicines and then arranged an ambulance and sent her to Guwahati. She was admitted to a corporate hospital, but it was too late. A vessel in her brain had burst and there was a lot of internal bleeding. Sumi could not be saved. She passed away within 2 days.

This unpredictable death of a youngster came as a very big shock to me not just personally, but also demoralised the team. There was such a sense of loss and sorrow around. It was a big blow to lose a good member so early in life. As a leader, I understood the challenge of overcoming grief. I could not express my personal sorrow, I had to remain strong and hold my team together. This reinstated the leadership role in me further. We managed as a team to work as usual and helped Sumi's parents. They were a poor family and we did whatever we could at that hour of grief to support them. Sumi still remains in our hearts and in 'Better Life' Paneri center, her death anniversary is still celebrated every year. Even if she left us, she is always in our prayers. These are events that fine tune an organisation's work culture, the bonding and how you treat your employees as one big family.

Another incident happened that taught me a lesson on how to tackle a rogue team member. We had a centre manager, a middle aged man, who was also a sales person for different networking businesses. He was very well versed with the villages around and he knew a lot of people and hence I employed him as a centre manager. One day he vanished with a lot of money and in those days, every Asha worker was paid commissions in cash as they did not accept online payments. These commissions were put in envelopes and given to the centre manager who distributed them. Every Sunday they used to get their money.

That week came with bad news. Many Asha workers started calling me on Monday morning, saying they did not get the commission and on probing we got to know the truth! This man had fled with the money. Not just duping us, he also created a lot of trouble for us in the market for the next 6 months. He kept his phones switched off, we could not track him down, but he went around bad-mouthing us. I don't know what instigated him, why he turned into an enemy from an employee. He was always treated well and held as an important part of our team.

This came as a big blow to the team and different members gave different opinions. When you have a small team, your dependency on the team is very high. So if one member gets corrupted, the whole rhythm of the team functioning gets hampered. It came as a leadership challenge to me. But I believe a leader keeps evolving through such difficult incidents and learns better through bad times, like I did. During such times keeping the team consolidated and their morals high and explaining and discussing with them, what they are feeling at such a juncture is very important for any leader.

- 5 -

I jumped to steer my team, my ship through rough waters. My leadership qualities were very instrumental at this juncture, the most important of all being 'Communication.' If a leader cannot communicate, a lot of problems will start and if you do not get to know them before others do, then you will fail.

The second important rule I followed was 'Be Fair To All.'

I had no bias. If I am judging a situation then the judgement has to be fair too. All employees are equal to me. I might have personal favourites, but that is outside the premise of 'Better Life.' Next came 'Putting my Team First.' In terms of priority, they are ahead of me.

I emphasized on the 3 pillars of Leadership:

Communication

Be Fair to All

Put your Team first

Then came the Preciousness and Value of Time. Respect for Time was pathetic in Assam. They use a word: 'Lahey Lahey' which means 'slow slow.' At times they are slower than a tortoise and extremely laid back. On the rural front, they are 100 times more laid back. But in the healthcare sector, the value of time is very important, every second counts when you are saving a patient's life. You must reach on time, attend on time, not keep anyone waiting. Your lunch can happen later, but the patient can't wait. This I found was very tough to instill, but it was a continuous process, and I kept on trying till I succeeded. Leadership is all about patience. You have to repeat the same thing a 1000 times. Many of them had low IQ, some could not come out of the culture they grew up in, and I knew I could not change them overnight. A lot of patience and persistence was required to lead them.

Leadership is like a commander on a battlefield. Everyone in the army can leave, but the commander will fight till the end. Similarly when you build an enterprise with your own sweat and grime, as the founder, you have to stick to the commitments, come what may. You have to show up everywhere and continue to fight and that did inspire some, if not everyone. More so they saw a woman fighting for the team. That was something inspiring specially in a place like Assam's rural belt where the woman hardly had a voice.

I have seen patients in my chamber where the husbands decided if they will buy the medication for the woman's illness or if she will undergo a procedure and the woman had to meekly accept the husband's decision. And I was doing everything opposite in a culture where the women were really dominated. So in that culture the team accepting a woman boss and seeing her lead from the front was difficult, yet achievable.

There were times when I spoke to team members one on one to build a relationship with them. Members came from different backgrounds. I also had a single mother, a nurse, fighting for a divorce from her abusive husband, yet wearing red vermillion to prove she was still married. She had a young boy to raise, and her fight against society, financial conditions, she stayed with her brothers, everything was like a movie. Then I had another young nurse who was a victim of domestic abuse. Every time she got pregnant, her child died inside the womb and her in-laws were frustrated as she could not give an heir to the family. I had a male employee who had sickle cell anemia while his daughter had thalassemia. He often fell sick and I had to support him and his daughter. I even donated blood during an emergency when an employee's sister was fighting for her life after an episode of severe bleeding.

Thus everyone had their own story of struggle and I as a leader had to play the supportive role for everyone. I had to know them personally, support them whenever and wherever they needed, be it celebrating an employee's child's birthday, or donating materials for their household. When they started realising I was not just paying them salary, but someone who stood by them during their hardships, they also extended their helping hands to me. So some of the employees actually turned into my family, and I was part of theirs.

We also celebrated an employee's birthday with cake cutting. They could never even think of it, they never imagined. Their immediate families also came and the celebration was like a VIP moment for them. They were photographed, loaded on social media. These small gestures for them were very touching. Thus caring for your team is a very big aspect for any leader. And I tried to do it all out for my team at 'Better Life.'

I realised that educating my team was of utmost importance. Education was the most important way of building a strong foundation for them. Thus started our series of weekly training sessions. I taught them everything - right from medical skills, communication skills, accounts and finance and even Excel sheets. We had sessions on financial planning helping them realize the importance of saving money the right way.

All my team members were malnourished. In the villages, they were never taught about nutrition and the correct ways of cooking. A malnourished mother was also raising malnourished children. I thus started cooking for them; this not only gave me a chance to bond with them over food but also helped me to teach them the recipes of such dishes which were essentially made of local ingredients that were easily available at affordable prices. One of the most successful dishes were Protein laddoos that I made with sattu, coconut, jaggery and ghee. They would eagerly wait for such days when I would carry food cooked by me in casseroles. I even fed some of them with my own hands when they would be sick. Somewhere the 'mother' in me was being nurtured by them.

We celebrated some specific days too like Doctor's Day, Nurse's Day etc, where we honoured and valued their services as healthcare professionals. I allowed my team members to give speeches and in a rural community that was a very big honour. They were allowed to speak for themselves, how they felt about being a healthcare professional and so on. Every month we also organised an 'Employee of the Month' competition and the winner got a special gift. One of the criteria of the competition was : 'What unique things did you do to bring a smile to a patient.' Such strategies in a way helped encourage creativity and efforts among employees and also brought about a vibrant environment at the centre.

They realised that as a healthcare professional they have much more responsibility than any other profession, something they did not know before and they are also respected more than others. Now they felt proud to be one. I remember this single mother nurse came to me one day and said when she returns home everyday on her scooty, wearing the nurse's dress, everyone looks at her with a lot of respect. She even thanked me and said that because of me, she feels she got a lot of respect.

Not just money, social standing and respect were very important for these people. The essence of being valued was so long missing in their lives, they came from a background wreaked in frustration, depression etc, and now they valued their lives, they felt motivated. This in turn gave me the biggest lesson in leadership — only money cannot add value, one needs a lot more than mere *roti, kapda, makan.* They needed respect and social recognition.

The First Team of Better Life

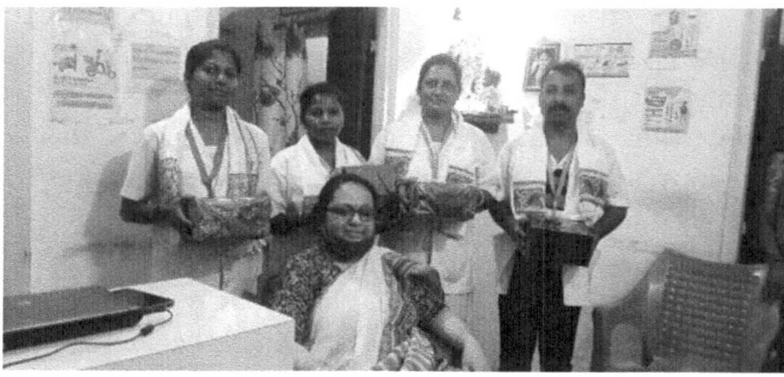

Recognizing the Best Employees

A Happy Team is the key to success

Empowering the Women of Better Life

Our beloved Sumi

Chapter 7

Tips for Budding Healthpreneurs

I do not mind sharing some tips with those who wish to set up Healthcare Business in any form. Remember all these tips come from a multitude of experiences I acquired in my chequered life as a doctor as well as while setting up and running Better Life. Hands-on experience taught me many new things that I never knew I would encounter. I would love to share with you all 10 such golden tips so that anyone setting up a business in this sector might be benefitted.

- Healthcare business is very different from any other business as it involves life and death of a human being. So no other business is so critical in terms of outcome. Hence every decision one takes has to be bang on. You cannot have flips and flops, no chance to be wrong. Else it can impact someone's precious life. It is thus better to enter this business only if you are ready to commit yourself to this criticality. For this is a 24x7 game, as a healthcare business owner, you may or may not be a doctor. Say you are a practising doctor like me, then all the time you cannot handle both the practice and the administration. So you have to be committed completely to the business through proper strategy, operational visions and everything else required to set the game straight. Only if you feel you are 100% ready, then take a plunge.

- In comparison to many other businesses, the core team of a healthcare business always needs to involve trained professionals, doctors, paramedics, pharmacists or even for the operation you need people trained and specially skilled to be in the OT. Since you need a specific kind of employee, their count is limited, hence they are difficult to get. To optimize your efforts and ensure the operation goes smoothly, retention of such trained employees is very important compared to any other business. So when you design your human resource policy, you have to keep in mind the retention factor, the policies you develop depend on budget, location, access to healthcare employees, but you cannot afford a lot of attrition in this business. You cannot afford to lose those you have trained and built as a team to face any emergencies. And emergencies are pretty common in this sector.

- You have to do a lot of PR, you do in all businesses in modern times. But in the current era, the healthcare business is somewhere on the edge. Though it is an essential service that everyone will need at some point of life, still most people want it to be a charity. So anything beyond their pocket even if that advice is correct, they will not take it and come up with complaints and bad-mouthing that can be detrimental to your business. People will label you as expensive and think you operate unnecessarily for money. That mentality of customers will always be there. So public relations is needed, invest money, strategy, knowledge etc into that, to form a loyal band of customers who will trust you. Then you will be able to stay afloat despite challenging situations. It involves good Samaritan activities like organising free health camps, community activities, working with local government authorities, political parties, police etc to give services to the masses. You have to build that image for sure. You cannot avoid it, good rapport with press and media, good reviews online, good social media presence and all of these count in making a social image for sure in present times.

- When you are chalking out the operation plan of your business, it is very important you have on board, healthcare experts, especially doctors experienced in the field along with administration experience, you need a lot of licences with specifications. Right from the time you are setting up your business to daily running. When you start giving service, you will realise, things which look petty are actually essential to jot down – how entry and exit of the business are designed, how doctors' chambers are designed, where the washroom is located etc. These issues otherwise might look small but they are very important from an operational viewpoint. And hence this calls for meticulous planning.

- Using proper technology is a must in today's world. We are in an age where you cannot work without technology. Even in a rural setup, just with an OPD based set up also you will need technology. Do not run away from it, buy good software, include tele medicine based technology in your setup; a significant dependency on tech can somehow help us ease out too much dependency on employees. You will need guidance regarding choosing the right technology, so consulting tech experts before installing a system is imperative.

- When you are off to start the business, draw a mission and vision plan, something different from any other healthcare business competitors. Though the basic thing remains the same – treatment of patients. But the USP of your healthcare business has to be different. Like we at Better Life were providing quality driven tech based healthcare services to the last mile patients but at affordable rates. So draw your USP, however simple it might be. Do a detailed competitor study to understand what they are doing and chalk out your plan accordingly.

- Innovation is prime. If you cannot incorporate new services and present old wine in a new bottle, then you succumb to competition. So design out special things like in case of 'Better Life' we always had discounts and offers, every month. Some combo offers to engage and encourage patients. Those who are loyal customers, they came up and asked themselves about our offers at the reception. They were so hooked to the element of offers. Innovation is important to thrive in the market.

- Most healthcare business owners think marketing in the case of their business is just about meeting other doctors, so marketing persons just go and meet fellow doctors asking them to refer patients and get a commission out of it. But healthcare marketing has an entire basket of things one needs to do – digital and traditional marketing to reach your end customer. To strategise that one needs an expert's help and like any other business, marketing is absolutely essential. You cannot lose it and strategies must encompass 360 degree coverage of all aspects.

- If you are the doctor as well as the owner of the business, you cannot afford to do everything on your own. If you are practising, then handling patients and administration together can be tedious. Those who are not doctors will also face challenges while running a healthcare business due to lack of medical experience. In both cases, team structure and hierarchy need to be defined and hence professionals are needed to handle. Else growth will be limited and you will burn out too soon. Organising a team's structure and hierarchy is very important and some specific areas can be kept under the wings of the founder. Rest work should be designated to experts in the field.

- A common misconception people have about healthcare businesses is that we earn a lot of money. It's true in a way, but there are many ifs and buts. Every healthcare business needs a lot of time as what we call the 'incubation period.' The time gap between starting a business and getting actual profits is long, so one has to have enough funds, patience and persistence to be able to keep going, correct calculations, and regular monitoring. Profit will not come overnight and one must be ready for it and be aware of the same before venturing into it. If one can innovate and keep the team in place, then definitely it is a profitable business as it is an evergreen business, a safe sector to be in but one has to keep the 'time' element in mind.

Working With the Local Asha and Anganwadi Workers to Create Impact

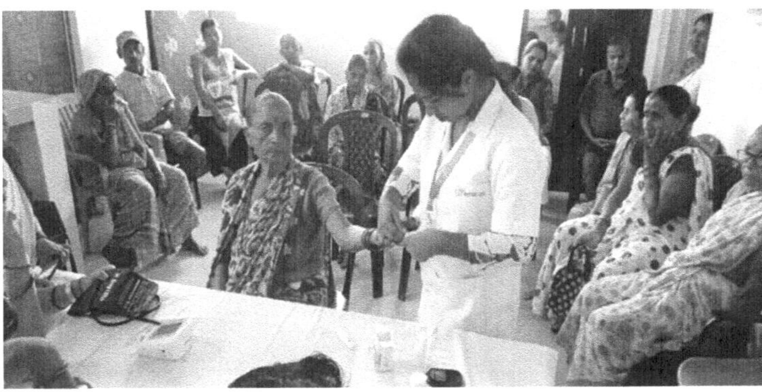

Health camps are a regular affair at Better Life

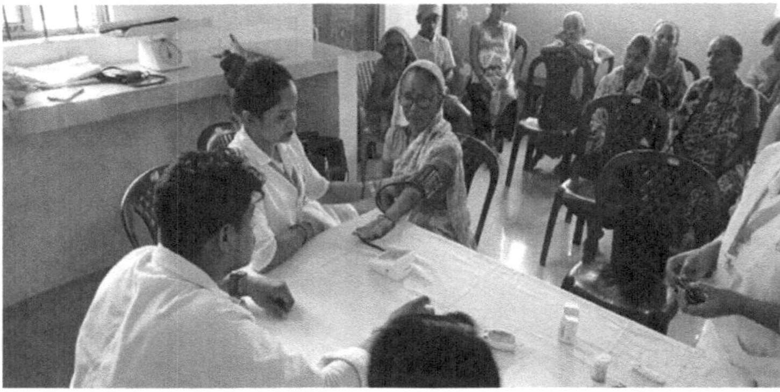

Women's Day health camp at Paneri

Health check up at the local Durga Puja pandal

Chapter 8

When I Challenged the Challenges

Like every champion, I was a challenger too, especially in the initial years of being an entrepreneur. When you challenge the challenges that come your way, see it eye to eye, then every challenge vanishes or makes way to solutions. For me as an entrepreneur working in a remote location, the challenges were far more than one setting up a business in an urban environment and ecosystem. The challenges also taught me life's lessons, I became more resilient, though at times I slipped and fell as well. I do not thus mind sharing the real life stories and challenges that an entrepreneur faces, no point sugar coating the same like an icing on the cake. An entrepreneur, not just has to bake the cake, she even has to hunt and fetch every ingredient that goes into making the same and even has to whip the cream that will go as the topping. I had to do it all, only then the delicious icing arrived.

I would thus wish to share the challenges that every entrepreneur faces in life. Remember you are not alone, and the ecosystem will do everything possible to break you, until you decide to make yourself a success story, just like I did. I do not wish to paint a hunky dory picture for any other entrepreneur, saying entrepreneurship is a great opportunity and so on. It is more of a deadly challenge and success comes much later, after a lot of investments — time, money, energy, vision and so on. Everything never falls in place, for me it didn't. It is very important to lay out the probable obstacles and multiple challenges one faces from beforehand. When somebody steps into entrepreneurship, everything will not always be perfect. These days we often speak of start-ups, being your own boss, not being run of the mill, having freedom, having money, not to be stuck in a 9-5 job etc. This is the outer cover of entrepreneurship to sugarcoat the concept and popularise the idea of entrepreneurship. No one talks of the hardships on social media. It is always the pretty picture that one gives. I think the concept is overhyped. It is always the opposite to what is presented.

- The biggest challenge I faced was working from a remote location. Finding the right place to start the business was a humongous challenge and so was arranging for the initial funds. Not just the working capital, an entrepreneur like me had to arrange for 6-9 months of capital for the business, pulling out money from one's own pocket to sustain the team and fixed costs like electricity, rent etc. Hence the entire planning depends hugely on the amount of funds one has and proper planning to use the same in a strategic manner. So arranging funds was the first hurdle for me. I left my cushy job, working as the medical super of a mother and child hospital of Guwahati and had a handsome salary. So the first question was where would I get funds if I wished to start 'Better Life?' This is the biggest obstacle for any entrepreneur. I invested from my own savings, partly funded from a bank loan. Getting a loan was another challenge since my business was not based in the city but in a remote location. So no banks were easy to convince that the business had prospects.

- Above that I was an entrepreneur doctor, so I had to present the best of my 'doctor' self too, to prove myself again and again and again that I was good for my patients and could pull them out from the jaws of death.

But that is not an easy game, it is not like buying and selling products, it is about human life, germs, infections, diseases, human bodies that can go wrong any minute even if you try your best. Say, I treated 100 patients successfully but that does not mean the 101th will go home fine. If one is not cured properly for reasons beyond my scope, then also people will attack you, negating your success stories of the previous 100 cases. So continuously proving my worth and efficacy as a doctor was a great challenge. But then again I am very grateful that I got the opportunity to prove myself in immensely challenging situations, treating critical patients in a rural setting and successfully sending them home.

- Then comes the challenge of tackling people around you. All are not the same. There are those who want to either take advantage or try to sabotage your efforts when you are successfully running a profitable business. There are people not interested in the monetary part but will always try to pull you down. If you are a woman entrepreneur, then you face even the patriarchal rant. So much is happening in the 21st century, in the age of AI, but in the Indian society's perspective, there still remains a divide between a man and a woman. In rural locations it is far pronounced and on the face. So as a woman entrepreneur, my job was more difficult.

- Another common challenge that every entrepreneur faces is how to recruit the right team. There is a myth about this. Most entrepreneurs think they have a vision about what kind of employee he or she will recruit and thus find the right one. But trust me we are working with humans, and not robots, so you will never get someone, let alone a bunch of people who will be upto your vision. Rather you have to train and build the team. Despite the investment, time, money etc. the one you train and turn into an asset, might leave your organisation without even giving notice! Strange? Well no. That is what happens in every trade. Some employees are more interested only in the salary and bonuses. They do not care about a good work environment or how well you treat them. Retaining them is a challenge. And it took me a lot of time and hard work to create the trust between me and my team, till they felt they needed to be part of the bigger vision of 'Better Life.' Still attrition was a reality and that was indeed a big challenge.

- Then comes the authorities or the local and state government mechanism. Without appreciating entrepreneurs like us who put up healthcare set ups providing better services than government clinics in remote areas like Paneri where I set up Better Life, they victimise us. The entire system is corrupt everywhere, bribery involves big time, rules are not followed, under qualified people run the show and they neither understand your vision, nor will let you work without hindrances. So this system is a continuous pain in the neck and it's a bigger problem in the rural set up as these people are not under the monitoring of the higher ups directly and they think in a rural system they are the boss and prime authority. Hence they pose a big problem. Fighting one's way through corruption and such a system is a big challenge.

- For me another challenge was the language barrier. Since I was not from Assam, it was a big issue. I had to speak that local language, even in the city, as well as rural areas. If you know the local language, you are more welcome. The problem was greater in my case as I was in a rural environment where most people did not know Hindi or even English. So I always had a nurse by my side seeing patients who would be my translator. Still patients would come and say "Oh doctor madam doesn't know Assamese? Then how will she explain it to us?" And that was a great barrier between me and them.

- The challenge of implementation of systems was huge specially in an area where I started my business. When you start your enterprise, by default you are doing everything from A to Z . If the founder is not well even one day then everything crumbles. Hence we entrepreneurs too need to change it. A founder cannot be sitting in one business all the time, rather he or she should sit 'on the business.' The team and employees need to follow the system, so that even if the founder entrepreneur is not present, things will still run smoothly. But employees have their own agenda and own way of looking at the system. When you are dealing with half educated people who are not tech savvy, their acceptance of a new idea, new concept etc itself is a big challenge. So it took a lot of effort to explain to them why a certain system was being introduced and how it could benefit them and patients alike. Monitoring the execution of a system whether it is working well or not, reviewing the same at intervals is a continuous cycle in the business. And trust me, it is a tedious job for sure.

- The final challenge that entrepreneurs often ignore is 'Me Myself.' As a founder you are juggling so many things that you get completely burnt out. You have no life, no social life, no friends and peers, no life at all apart from work. Since we gave 24x7 services and though employees went home after work, I couldn't. Often this extreme hard work with absence of social life, took a toll on me. I did feel like quitting. It is something commonly faced by all entrepreneurs. That was the time I always thought about the purpose, the core mission of 'Better Life,' to provide services to the underprivileged, that basic reason kept me going and helped me to hold on whenever I got impatient. The only key to success I believe is persistence. That keeps you going.

Building the inclusive culture at Better Life

Dr Bhattacharjee addressing a press conference at the Guwahati Press Club

Inauguration of the pickup and drop services for patients - first-ever in that area

Chapter 9

Expanding Horizon

- 1 -

When Better Life was around two years old, I started contemplating an expansion plan. We already had patients coming from different districts, other than Udalguri — like Barpeta, Rangiya, Mangaldoi, Sonitpur, even from distant Arunachal Pradesh bordering districts. All these areas were about 50-100km away from our Better Life Paneri centre. This in a way reflected our achievement too, as our service quality and success rate in making sick people healthy again was super and that news spread far and wide. My Better Life model was working and reaching far off places. These were our fruits of labour and most of these patients from other areas heard good things about us and were keen to be treated at our centres. They did not come through advertisements. This was a great success for my team as well. Better Life was now a household name to reckon.

I started sharing the expansion plans with my team as I had always been a democratic leader and wished for their feedback too. Along with that began the recce of different places where we can start our next centre or centres and further branches of Better Life. We zeroed down on 3 locations – around 35-50 km away from Better Life Paneri, and they were in different directions. Planning a location needs proper strategic planning. The growing network of Better Life was strategically planned already – that was evident while we put in place the expansion plans.

One cannot just choose any location as per his or her choice. It has to be planned in advance taking into account various dynamics like competitor and customer dynamics of that particular location. When we see with a macro eye, all patients look the same, they are all sick, they are all from the same community etc. But when you dig deep, you realise there is a lot of difference between the people of different localities and accordingly their needs as well. We studied all this, I travelled extensively, met the natives of these places, took some of them on board, so that I got a first hand account of the local dynamics that was very important to set up any of the new centres that I was planning.

- 2 -

Then came the challenge of arranging funds. Some came from my savings, but to a large extent it was arranged by bank loans. And needless to say there were lots of challenges in getting the loans as I was working in a remote area and most banks did not have their branches in those locations. So convincing the banks to come to Paneri and see the infrastructure of Better life and our model needed a lot of convincing. They had to believe in our vision that we supplied essential medical services to the masses in such remote locations and bank loans would be helpful in doing that — we had to make them believe what we were doing on ground. It was a journey of perseverance and patience.

And we reaped the rewards soon. Once loans were arranged, it was all about replicating the 'Better life Paneri' model. So from the blue print to interior plans to applying for the licenses – all these were done again while opening the healthcare business. By then some of my team members from Paneri who were trained and were working with me for the last two years, had turned good enough and became the 2nd line of leaders for our organisation. They could take up bigger team responsibilities and were efficient enough in leading smaller teams as well.

I felt now that when the business was of a single unit, it was easier to micro plan. This is true for any enterprise — be it a clinic or shop or any establishment, we need proper systems in an organisation to run it smoothly when it grows. In a single unit system, it is much easier to microplan, supervise, monitor on a daily basis by the founder. During expansion, the founder's vision has to have a macro vision and ability to see all the multiple units at the same time. For that proper systems need to be implemented. And from day one, I knew this would help in the long run and hence implemented these systems well in advance, everything was planned, written, and this time I decided to make a SOP or Standard Operating Procedure Manual which had descriptions with details about each department and every activity under each department. I feel this is a must for any organisation specially for healthcare. The computerised system, the softwares used etc, everything is part of the system. And this helps to transfer the knowledge to juniors who can then pass them on to the next level. So the entire system of hierarchy and sharing knowledge down the chain existed.

I had to recruit a lot of new people which was a bit chaotic in the beginning, but again the system came to my rescue. Some of my previous team members showed a lot of leadership skills at this hour and all our hard work in training them was finally paying off. A lot of new centre work was being handled by the old staff, that came as a relief to me. But challenges were galore, especially the local political goons. Some wanted money, some created trouble otherwise. Even some ex-team members were trying to create some kind of ruckus to jeopardise the expansion plan. Achievements and challenges go hand in hand and any leader has to take it in their stride.

- 3 -

And that stride at times comes with a pinch of salt, and at times with a lot of fun. The mantra is to find positivity in everything and keep up the team spirit. There were many funny incidents during this time. I remember we had to go to a Gaon Burra of a locality, where we were coming up with a new project and getting his signature on a form for the trade license was needed. Now this man did not know how to read and write and which form was to be signed by him, most days he would lie in his house dead drunk. So we had to take help from his wife to get him aligned and go to the Panchayat to get the form and after multiple rounds of visit to his house, we achieved it. The signature came, also in the form of a thumb print! Things get thus delayed in such remote locales.

It is a kind of test for every founder, at every step, when you will find such non-cooperative people and such situations. If you give up then your entrepreneurship journey just stops there. You have to find means and ways to navigate through every crisis and bumps on your way. But if you can go ahead facing these challenges, you will certainly win. And I was celebrating these wins with my team as well. Their hard work had to be appreciated.

I realised with so many branches coming up, we needed a better inventory management system of the Pharmacy. We usually bought stocks from Guwahati or other states and channelised them to Paneri's pharmacy. But once you have multiple branches, the pharmacy inventory with 1000 plus product SKUs also requires proper maintenance.

That was a tedious job. We had such a huge variety of stocks and hence it was very difficult without proper inventory software. I had good software running, but now I had to start a centralized medicine warehouse as well, near Guwahati airport. I invested in a more robust pharmacy software that was also used by one of the top online pharmacy providers of India. Recruiting and training people to use that software was another challenge. But the centralised warehouse was established and a beautiful supply chain was created where all stocks came to the centralized warehouse, sorted there, barcoded there and different branches could place their orders to this centralised warehouse and then their stocks were sent according to the orders placed.

This was a brilliant system and ensured medicines reached on time to branch pharmacies that were our retail outlets also. No expiry date medicines were there, minimal wastage, optimisation of time was taken care of. We designed a logistic system where the local public buses coming from remote centres to Guwahati were used to pick up the stock from the centralized warehouse.

- 4 -

Once the Better Life branches were launched, they had individual requirements on what was working and what was not working for that particular centre. Just like all fingers of a hand are not of same size and shape, you cannot expect all centres to be running on the same wavelength. They will have their own local issues, problems, positive and negative sides too.

So I introduced both common and individualized activities of the branches, based on local dynamicities, and thus certain specific marketing activities had to be arranged. That included community activities that we had already done in Paneri. The experience we got in Paneri was extremely useful. So I advise future healthcare entrepreneurs that they should ensure the first unit they start is perfect, so that during expansion, one can just replicate the first unit. Then it becomes easier when you branch out on a bigger scale.

There were a lot of challenges even after the branches were launched, but we took care of everything. A proper human resource hierarchy is important too. When you have the right kind of people in your organizations and they can take up responsibilities on your behalf, then the smooth running of multiple branches is ensured. We also introduced a system of audits that my team had never heard of and initially there was a lot of resistance when the first time auditors came. Gradually they understood the importance of audits and it taught them why honesty is required in such organizations and that one cannot be dishonest and cheat the founder. Thereafter audit became important to Better Life and we had both internal and external audit teams.

So I shall emphasize on:

- A proper trained human resource hierarchy
- Adequate systems which can run on an auto pilot mode
- Overall system of monitoring and reviews by building a framework of planning, implementation, monitoring, review and again planning as a process cycle. An organisation can run very well if this cycle is followed.

That's how an entrepreneur can easily spread their wings to multiple areas and still script a success story by overcoming all challenges.

Team Better Life at the Inauguration of our 3rd unit

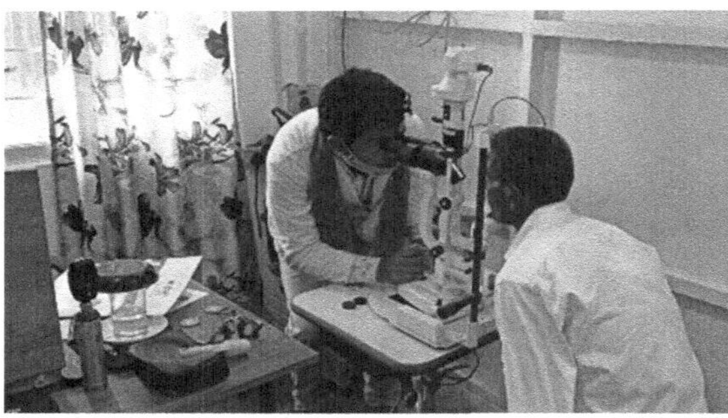

Eye care facilities at Better Life

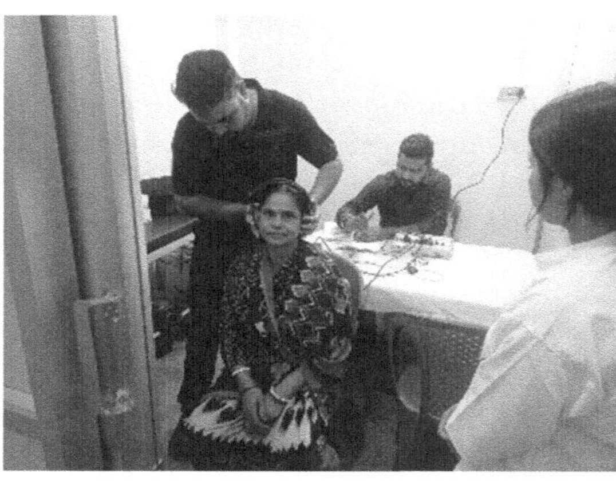

Hearing related assistance at Better Life

Chapter 10

My Journey Ahead

- 1 -

There are times when people do not challenge themselves and hence are unaware of their own strengths. I feel every person should take up new challenges and extend oneself beyond one's comfort zone to see how much we can give. Through Better Life's journey, I realised there is immense patience and persistence in me, that probably I had lost somewhere on the way, through my personal losses in life. But Better Life reinstated that in me. When you undergo your own entrepreneurial journey, you realise everything is not going to happen to you instantly. You have to learn to wait for the right things to happen and this waiting period is extremely difficult sometimes as it tests your patience a lot. But if you can go through it then you are the winner. I have learnt so many profound lessons including lessons in leadership, art of team building and much more.

When you deal with people who are not skilled, to pick them up from their basics, you have to surrender to the process, bow down to their situations, leave all your own achiever's ego behind. Only then can you pick up somebody who is sitting at the bottom and one day becomes an asset for your organisation. This was an immense lesson to me. I think 'Better Life' will always be a very important foundation of the person that I am today and I wish to carry on this journey, if this becomes a legacy, it will be another feather in the cap, but a journey none the less. A journey that will be lived for the underprivileged, for people who have basic life needs, who have no access to a lot of luxury that we can afford, yet they choose to live. The minimum that educated people like us can do for them is to support them as much as possible.

- 2 -

When I look back at my journey, I think about a lot of things. One pertinent question that keeps looming large in my head is through whatever I have done in my profession or in my life, there was always this quintessential search. I was searching for something, whether be in the remote islands of Sundarbans, or the lanes of Sonagachhi, or remote tea gardens in Assam and Darjeeling, or through the entire entrepreneurial journey of 'Better Life,' through the corporate lanes of hospitals and pharmaceutical companies, I was definitely searching for that 'Purpose of Life.'

Somewhere subtly the question remained and it took me a lot of time to understand that the purpose of my life was service. Many people equate doctors with service, but practically that is not true. Not every doctor believes in service. For me, it has always been that selfless service and that is the only thing that quenches my thirst. So throughout my professional journey, the vision I had was taking me from one zone of service to another. In 'Better Life' I completed that cycle. Now I wish to be known for providing service and establishing healthcare at the last mile.

So through my recent venture 'KliniZen Healthcare Ventures and Consulting.' I want to help people who want to start similar healthcare units in their own localities, especially remote areas. I want to help them right from ideation to the grand launch, what we technically call as idea to commissioning and also hand hold them through their journey.

Healthcare business is very different from other businesses as it gives you an opportunity for a life with purpose. Besides being a business per se, of course there will be profit loss, strategy etc, but at the end of the day you are providing service to a sick person, a person who is in pain and what more satisfaction can one really experience when that person gets relief. Every single night on my 'Better Life' journey, I used to think of all my patients – their grief, agony, pain, physical and mental pain. When a patient after many days of agony got relief with the medicines that I gave, it gave me such a satisfaction. Nothing gives me a better kick than that.

- 3 -

Now I want to use my experience and expertise to build healthcare businesses particularly in remote areas, where there is huge need and demand. Very few people dare to set up something like 'Better Life' and through 'KliniZen' I want to take it to the next step. I am also working on a venture which will cater to comprehensive wellness services for cancer patients. Cancer is a big danger looming large these days and other than chemotherapy, radiation, operation etc, there is a sense of complete healing for such patients other than just medicines. Irrespective of the ventures, all will revolve around good service to people who need it. That will help me live my life of purpose. The entire journey of 'Better Life' has been more of a journey within.

'Better Life' started as a challenge to me as no one supported me when I started. Everyone had doubts, some even said: What happens if your business fails? Who will be your back up if your business fails? Why go to a remote area? Why start business in an area famous for insurgency?

But I listened only to my soul calling that finally led me on my intense journey within and outside. And all that I experienced through it, I grew more resilient and stronger from within. Sometimes you need to fight against your own inhibitions and prejudices. You may or may not be bothered with the outside world. But you have to fight your own self doubts. Every patient I treated, every story I came across, every challenge I faced and every solution that I achieved were all ice breakers for me.

Somewhere deep within, I had a lot of knots that got untied as I went along my road to success. I am indebted to 'Better Life' for making me a better person. The element of compassion to understand another person's story and extending a hand of support to somebody else is so rare these days. And when you go to a remote location and you do not have the luxury, you go back to the basics of life. In a place where the internet was not available, electricity was off most of the time, and you still survive there, then you realise you can do anything on earth. For basic living you do not need luxuries. Imagine basic services like courier, receiving a parcel, was also a tedious job, things did not reach us in 10 minutes, even a parcel did not come to Paneri directly, you had to go 10 km to collect it. So when you do that you realise, life can also be like this.

I also for the first time got the opportunity of reading Bhagavad Gita while I was reinventing from within. I invested in skill development personally during this journey, like I learnt driving, a skill that came very handy to me. I turned vegetarian, a revolutionary change in my life, and learnt the art of minimalism, in both personal and professional life. You can serve and treat a patient, do good work with minimal resources. Also I am devoted to the art of organisation, I was always an organised person but when you are wearing multiple hats and you have patients and employees dependent on you, you have to be better organised.

Better Life was thus a very important journey within and it elevated me to a different plane for sure. In search of a better life, I created its namesake.

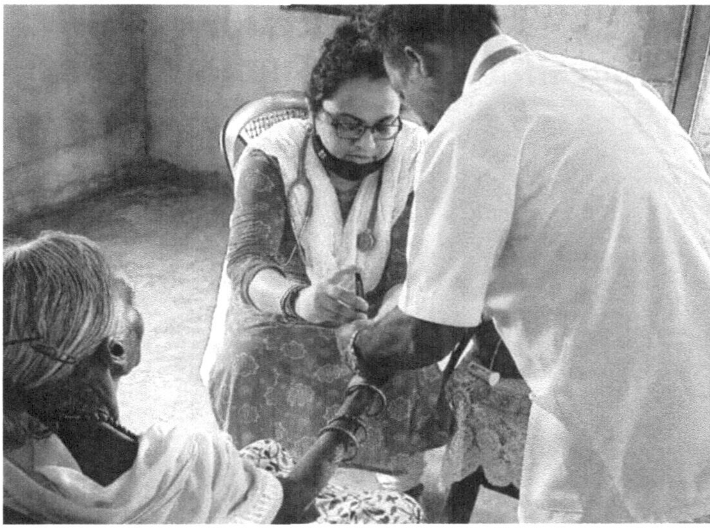

The healer within me has always stood the test of time

Eastern Chronicle

2 | FRIDAY, GUWAHATI SEPTEMBER 1, 2023

Students Chronicle

REACH FOR THE STARS

Transforming Rural Healthcare: Dr. Sayantani Bhattacharjee's Vision

Dr. Sayantani Bhattacharjee is a seasoned healthcare professional with over two decades of leadership experience across several organizations in the healthcare domain. Besides MBBS and a post graduate degree in Obstetrics and gynaecology from Calcutta University, she also possesses an MBA in Healthcare Management from AIHA, Hyderabad and a Fellowship in Adult & Child Psychology from NHCA, Singapore.

She is the founder of Better Life - Healthcare at the Last Mile. This organization was established in February 2021 during the COVID times. Better Life works in the rural areas of Assam to bring quality driven, comprehensive, affordable and accessible healthcare to all through its technology enabled one-of-its-kind medical centres. Here beneficiaries are offered a variety of primary healthcare services like free doctor consultation, diagnostics, day care facilities, eye care, ambulance, vaccination, healthcare packages, emergency care and pharmacy, all under the same roof.

Fuelled by her personal experiences, Dr. Sayantani addressed the critical issue of inadequate rural healthcare during the pandemic. She aimed to provide affordable, accessible, convenient, sustainable, and quality-driven primary healthcare services.

Fuelled by her personal experiences, Dr. Sayantani addressed the critical issue of inadequate rural healthcare during the pandemic. She aimed to provide affordable, accessible, convenient, sustainable, and quality-driven primary healthcare services. Her innovative "Polyclinic" concept, offering comprehensive services under one roof, has garnered attention, ensuring immediate treatment without relying on logistics. One of the company's standout features is free doctor consultation for a year with a nominal subscription fee, a game-changer for rural patients. Technological integration, advanced equipment, and a focus on service excellence set her venture apart.

Dr. Sayantani nurtures the dream of having similar footprints of good healthcare across the North East and East India. She has also been the recipient of many awards for her incredible work such as 'Champion of Cause' at the MSME Honours (East) 2023; 'Best Woman Entrepreneur' at the Bengal Leadership Awards 2023; 40 Under 40 Passionate Women leaders in Healthcare 2023; India Social Impact awards 2022; Influential Women Leaders in Business 2022; India's 100 under 40 by Fox Story India; The Real Superwoman Award 2022 by Forever Star India; Entrepreneur of the Year 2021 (Healthcare) and many more.

Navigating the male-dominated industry posed challenges, but Dr. Sayantani persevered, challenging norms and striving to be a role model for women in entrepreneurship. She emphasizes the need to value oneself, urging aspiring female entrepreneurs to believe in their worth.

Editorial Desk Students Chronicle

Coverage by the EASTERN CHRONICLE Newspaper

MEET THESE UNSTOPPABLE WOMEN FROM
THE EAST AND NORTH-EAST,
WHO ARE MAKING A REMARKABLE IMPACT
IN THEIR RESPECTIVE FIELDS

Coverage by the FEMINA Magazine (Sept 2023)